Living in the Grey

WEAM ZABAR

Dear Pao,

I hope this book touches your heart as much as your friendship touched mine.

With Love,
Weam

TABLE OF CONTENTS

Preface 1
1 Childhood 6
2 What's in a name? 17
3 Grief 25
4 Religion 33
5 Spirituality 40
    Meditation/Energy Healing 40
    Yoga 53
6 Mindfulness 65
    What the mind is 65
    Mindfulness in practice 79
    Presence 80
    Affect 83
    Perspective 83
7 Therapy 87
8 Surrender 98
    Surrender in Spirituality 100
    Surrender in Life 101
    Surrender at work 103
    Surrender at selfless service 107

9 Relationships 109
    Idealisation and Devaluation 113
    Triggers 116
    The Repair 118
10 A Life Worth Living 120
    Autonomy 121
    Competence 123
    Relatedness 124
    Final Thoughts 124
Acknowledgements 127

Preface

I called this book "Living in the grey" because finding a middle path has taken me the longest. I still struggle to gauge what is OK, what is overboard, what is too little. I tiptoe around what feels to me like a very thin line of grey when almost everyone else seems to be living in a field of it. Even writing this book, I find myself holding back, trying to strike a balance between vulnerability and self-preservation. An internal battle between bearing my soul, pouring my heart and getting completely naked, and getting paranoid, protecting myself and keeping my disorder a secret.

This is an external manifestation of the love in my heart pouring out to all the people diagnosed with borderline personality disorder out there. To say the one thing that your childhood self has missed, the thing that might have saved you from this disorder in the first place: I see you, I hear you, I understand you, I love you.

This is a mediator between the borderline and loved ones. This is to explain what you struggled to understand. To free you of responsibility for the parts of the relationship that your borderline beloved has brought into the dynamic, whilst at the same time giving you a lens from which you can view those behaviours and still see the immense love that they have.

This is a translator of the borderline experience. For the curious, the healers, the therapists and the humans who have enough compassion, a drive for inclusion and a willingness to connect.

This is for everyone. Because from my own borderline experience, there is nothing about the borderline emotional landscape that is foreign to anyone. We are scared of being abandoned by those we love, we sometimes feel too much, find it hard to soothe ourselves, think in black and white, suffer immensely, love deeply, push people we love away, beg people to stay, and downright get too much even for ourselves.

This is for me. This is the most healed version of my narrative that has been worked on for over a decade. A version that I hope will continue to evolve, transform, heal and make meaning of the mess it is to be borderline.

So when I tell her I'm borderline, she says: Oh She asks me if it's like bipolar, asks me about Girl Interrupted, asks me if I'm crazy, I get that a lot I say: No crazy is not a clinical term

She asks me what it feels like and I tell her it's feeling nothing and everything all at the same time It's walking around like this world like it's black or white there is no middle, I drink too little, or too much Eat more than I should, drink more than I want to and burn bridges faster than I can build them But my God do I still build them, just without the truth

I tell her I'm not a sociopath, I'm not dangerous

It's only my skin, that is paper thin and breaking, I tell her that I love her I beg her not to leave

My world is a house of cards, carefully manipulated

...Precariously perched

But I can't open the door or the whole thing will cave

She asks me What the fuck do I mean when I say borderline, then? So I tell her:

Frantic efforts to avoid real or imagined abandonment One of my only clear childhood memories is when my babysitter left without saying goodbye

I watched her leave through the blinds of my window thinking she didn't love me anymore tears streaming down chubby cheeks

I remember crawling onto my toy chest in the closet And crying myself to sleep

I was four, it was late, I was supposed to be sleeping

A pattern of unstable or intense relationships characterised by alternating between extremes of idealisation and devaluation

My mama says I fall in love with my friends

I introduce myself with my heart on my sleeve

beating love me, love me, love me

because I love you, I love you, I love you

but hurt me and I'll do more damage than you can imagine

My heart will turn into ice

my mouth will become a matchbox,

one strike and I will ignite you, letting the heat of

your fire thaw me for the next round

Identity disturbance

Markedly and persistently unstable sense of self

When I look in the mirror sometimes a stranger stares back at me

Alone, late at night, I have no idea who I am, I am floating, my feet high above the ground

When they call me by my name sometimes it takes me a second, a day, a week before I answer

Recurrent suicidal gestures, behaviours or threats Mama says I was eight, the first time I wrote out my own suicide notes

There was one for my parents, for my best friends for my dog

It's not that I don't remember why I wanted to die

I just sometimes forget why I wanted to live

Transient stress related paranoia or severe dissociative symptoms

When I'm left alone too long my heart beats faster than humming birds' wings

So I lock the door, so I check it three times, so I check it three times, so I check it three times,

But the funny thing about running from the boogie man Is you can't lock yourself out of your mind

You can't run from this, I tell her.

It always finds me in the end

So she hears all of this, smiles

and she takes a step back

I get that a lot.

I Have a Sparkling Personality (Disorder) - Alex Lane

1 Childhood

Let me draw you a very sketchy picture of what a borderline's childhood narrative sounds like:

There are things in my childhood that I remember so vividly: the way an air-conditioned room smelled in our old childhood home, feeling aggravated by having to have lunch every single day, the feeling of sun hitting my legs through our living room window, the smell of kebab that my mom grilled in our extremely tiny backyard for Friday lunch.

My childhood memories are fragmented. Some are completely missing from my mind, making it difficult for me to piece my childhood story in an easily relatable, coherent way. And I find that sometimes as I try to recollect my childhood story, my mind zaps; it hits the break so hard without me actually knowing what made it do that.

There have been psychiatrists that assumed that I had gone through a form of physical childhood trauma: physical abuse, molestation or neglect. I haven't. I was brought up by two loving, compassionate parents that made a very conscious decision to bring me into this world. Parents that did their best in every moment of my childhood.

I mention this because being borderline can definitely stem from childhood trauma, but our understanding of what trauma is needn't be physical, nor is it necessarily about how the parents were (although it certainly is the case sometimes). It sometimes stems from the temperament of the child too. Within the same household and being brought up by the same parents, it is rare that siblings get borderline together.

What I remember of my childhood is more of how I felt. I had this constant nagging feeling that something horrible was about to happen. I once forgot to do my homework when I was seven. I was watching my favourite TV show at the time, Full House, which played once a week around dinner time. When I remembered that I had forgotten to do my homework, it felt as though my soul dropped into my belly. It felt like terror, like there was a big consequence to this forgetting. This sinking feeling I had in my belly then continues to live within me now, bringing me a pre-empted warning (although those warnings are often false) that something bad is about to happen.

There wasn't a big consequence for forgetting to do my homework. My mother might have displayed disappointment, and in an adult's eye, no big deal. To my child self, it was. Her disappointment was terrifying; it made me freeze. I later understood, when I went to therapy, that this freeze was shame. I found it so difficult not to be frozen in shame when I did something wrong. I did not know then that what I did and who I was are to separate things.

It wasn't just shame. I found that once my feelings escalated, it was hard to come back down. Self-soothing was a foreign concept that I had not thought about until I started the inner work I discuss in this book. My ability to self-soothe was something that I had to consciously work on for a long time, and I still do.

I found it difficult to fall asleep. My sisters would be fast asleep before the first story my mom told was over. I, on the other hand, kept nudging my mom out of dosing off to tell me the rest of the story, then a second, then a third. My sleep was light, I spoke in my sleep, and still do when stressed. My parents were used to me sleep walking. I would walk down the stairs from my bedroom and do all sorts of weird things. I had visual auditory hallucinations when I was stressed, I still do sometimes, although they are more of sounds and smells now.

I remember that I was hyperactive. No amount of moving was enough for me. I moved so much during the day that my dad massaged my feet while I slept, saying that surely such small feet could not handle such a big demand. There was an insatiable thirst, a constant FOMO that there were not enough hours of the day for all the exploring I needed. School classes were boring; it felt too easy. I came second in my class every year till high school without trying. I had so much energy left in me by the end of the day that when my mom told my sisters and me bedtime stories, I would still be up begging for more stories while my sisters happily dozed off.

I remember feeling that I wasn't enough. I am intelligent, funny, curious. I was the family clown. There was always something new I wanted to try. But there was an emptiness inside of me that continued to grow the older I got. An emptiness that I still feed and hope to fill by overworking myself, extending myself too much, spreading myself too thin, burning myself out and cramming my schedule with tasks that are impossible to fit in one day. For years, I have tried to be too many things for too many people to fill that emptiness, and it still lurks in the background some days.

They say that abandonment is a borderline's greatest fear. My first recollection of actual abandonment was when I was in the sixth grade. My best friend "broke up" with me, saying she wanted her "freedom" to have other friends. Was I overbearing even then? Was I too much? Did I demand too much closeness? I'll never know. What I do know is that the pain was so immense that it stayed with me for months. That I replayed that moment in my head for a very long time. The way a veteran plays war, reliving it and being terrorised by it. Abandonment to me was trauma, my biggest fear, the one thing to be avoided at all costs. When it did happen, it felt a lot like PTSD. When the vibrations of her words "I want my freedom" hit my eardrums, the pain was so awful I checked out. I dissociated. I left my body, and my mind, and zoned out.

This is something I learned to do very early on. To exit when it got too much. I remember feeling this way whenever one of my parents lectured me about something. I would just look into their faces until the room blurred and moved and swirled around me. And their faces would start looking disproportionate. Colours would change right before my eyes. It would send a tingling feeling all around my body, and I just wasn't there anymore. And so it didn't hurt as bad. Dissociation feels a little like a nightmare: you don't know what's happening, you have no control over what's going on, but somehow, the danger isn't as threatening as real life.

Of course, I did not know what it was called, or that it was a thing, or why I did it. It was something I discovered in my thirties, in a hypnotic state, in my therapist's office. But that's another story for another time (more specifically, in the therapy chapter).

When I did not dissociate, it felt like the alternative way to deal with painful reality is to get angry. The kind of anger that would have you black out. Saying things you would never imagine yourself saying or being violent in ways that would make you feel even more ashamed. My sisters would recall words I had said that I had no recollection of. It felt as though I was dodging being held accountable for my words when I genuinely had no recollection in some instances.

As an adult now, I see that I truly felt heard and taken seriously as a child when I was furiously angry. Anger was my way out of the pain of feeling so powerless, so unimportant, so unseen. The fact that my caregivers responded well to my anger made it a coping that I used for a long, long time.

I was hyper-social as a child. I could hardly spend any time alone. The silence sounded too loud for my liking, too terrifying to bear. I could be immersed in my internal world for hours without noticing, but I needed someone to be there in the background as a safety net.

I wanted to make friends, lots of them, and I did. The thought that someone did not actively like me wasn't something I was willing to tolerate. The pain of rejection was a strong fuel for the friend-making process. So I went out of my way to make friends, to make jokes, to connect.

I had healthy curiosity, the kind you would find in an intelligent, secure and mentally stable child. I often rebelled against family rules (although, more often than not, in a very harmless way) to fulfil that curiosity. I was a bit of a tomboy, I loved roller skating. And although we weren't allowed to play outside (read: overprotective parents), I would roll up the carpets of our living room when my parents had their afternoon siesta and roller-skate for hours.

I had a tiny yellow bike at home, one with training wheels that I had grown too big for when I was seven or eight. I begged my parents for a big girl's bike, a larger one with no training wheels. They refused. You did not buy toys for no reason those days. It would have to be a birthday, or the day you got your score card, something special, to get a new toy like that.

So I waited for my parents to have their siesta every day; I would sneak into my father's toolbox, take out the training wheels myself, practice riding my bike and then put them back on again before they woke up. This stayed a secret; I did not tell them what I was up to, as I knew they would be too worried that I'd hurt myself. So I waited until I mastered riding a bike. The day I felt confident, I called them and proudly showed them what I could do. They were both proud and mortified. I did not have to wait for my birthday. They saw my obsession and bought me a 20" blue BMX shortly afterwards.

My mother would take us with her to the yacht club a couple of times a week. She would roll into the gym, and our nanny would take my younger sister and me into the playground. I would do flips and tricks on the monkey bars, get dizzy on the merry-go-round, see how fast I could go on the seesaw, swing as high as I could, then jump off. When it was hot, we would swim in the pool. I would get so hungry on those days that the dinner we got, always a burger and chips, was one of the very few meals I actually enjoyed as a child.

My relationship with food was always a difficult one. I did not get hungry; I got angry, specifically every time lunch was served. It was so painful and boring for me to have lunch every day. My parents said I was not allowed to leave the table until my plate was empty. So I sat on the table for hours on some days, while I resorted to hiding what was left of my food away on other days. My mother was told that I would eat if I was hungry. To test that theory, she let me have it my way. I went three days without food, and my mother caved in and went back to force-feeding me.

Most of my childhood was what you would call "normal", although I'm not sure what that means anymore. Both my parents were educated, they both worked. My mother dedicated her life to take care of us; there was very little time that she wasn't around, probably running an errand. When she was home, she was almost always doing something. There was always a new hobby that she was obsessing over, always a busy bee. My father worked a double shift, so we only spent time with him on weekends where he would take us to a park or to the supermarket for treats. Although he did make a point of dropping off and picking us up from school every day so that he would have that riding time with us.

My parents' marriage aged like fine wine. What I see in them now is what I hope to have with a loving partner in old age. My parents fell in love when my father was studying abroad in Baghdad. After years, and many proposals (which were rejected by my grandfather, my mother's father, initially), my mother moved to Bahrain to be married to my father.

This is not an autobiography, and so I am not sharing all of this to tell you my life story but to address something very crucial in the borderline experience. Borderline Personality Disorder is a childhood trauma-based mental illness. Having read this snippet of my story, you could assume that I had it pretty good: two present and well-meaning parents, emotional support, financial security, two great siblings, lots of friends. What trauma, right?

After years of self-enquiry, therapy, Yoga, meditation, spirituality, religion and an awful lot of hours contemplating life, ethics, the universe, God, the reason for our existence and a whole other bunch of subjects that will make your head spin, here is what I understand now: I wasn't neglected, I had the perception that there was a threat that I would be. As a child, I saw that my mother carried deep sadness for being away from her family. My child mind made this about me. That my mother was sad because I wasn't good enough to make her happy. And I tried to. I did exceptionally well at school, I didn't ask for things I knew my parents could not provide, and I tried to avoid causing trouble where I could help it. But my mother was still sad. In my child's mind, this meant that I wasn't enough; if I had been enough, my mother would have been content with being with us. This filled me with fear of the possibility that I would one day wake up and she would be gone. That she would have been so sad and lonely that she could not take it, and she would up and go. Even as I write this now, I am filled with compassion towards my child self. I wish I could get down on my knees, look at the child me in the eyes and say, "This is not on you; you are enough. It is going to be okay".

And I want to say that I'm one of the lucky ones. After all, 87% of people who had been diagnosed with BPD have had severe childhood trauma or neglect. If I did that, though, I would be invalidating the feelings and experiences of BPDs that have had similar stories to mine. Perception of neglect has a very similar effect, psychologically speaking, to actual neglect. What makes perception of neglect very tricky is that there is no way to deal with something that has not actually happened. How can you be angry with a parent that had done their best?

And so here is the grey when it comes to my childhood:

My parents are human beings. They are not perfect; they are flawed. They are allowed to make mistakes and be forgiven for them. They can come down from their pedestal now. I free them from having to be perfect for me. They have had their own stories as children. They have misunderstood too, and been wounded. They did their best, and their best wasn't always enough.

I misunderstood much of what was going on around me because my brain as a child wasn't capable of understanding it accurately. For a while, I chose to continue to misunderstand because I did not know any better. Even when I wasn't a child anymore, I refused to understand sometimes because it felt too scary to change.

My understanding of what it takes to be a parent only crystallised when I became a mother myself. The emotional, mental and physical demands of being a mother changed the entitled narrative into a compassionate one. There is no blame in my heart for my parents; there is only love, understanding, compassion and gratitude. If I could do this life all over again, I would choose them once more.

"They fuck you up, your mum and dad. They
may not mean to, but they do. They fill you
with the faults they had And add some extra,
just for you.

But they were fucked up in their turn
By fools in old-style hats and coats,
Who half the time were soppy-stern
And half at one another's throats.

Man hands on misery to man.
It deepens like a coastal shelf.
Get out as early as you can,
And don't have any kids yourself."

– Philip Larkin, High Windows

2 WHAT'S IN A NAME?

Borderline is a name that was picked for this childhood trauma disorder as borderline was seen as the state between sanity and insanity. Until recently, borderline was not seen through the lens of the trauma but through an array of symptoms that might have been perceived as an "in-between" state by the untrained eye to the trauma.

I personally do not like the "personality disorder" part of the name either. It implies a choice of character when I see it more similar to a Post Traumatic Stress Disorder (PTSD) than a character flaw. Let's explore the symptoms of borderline with the understanding and through the lens that the symptoms are a result of childhood trauma, neglect, or threat of neglect:

- Mistrust of others, paranoia: if my caregiver was not reliable, how can anyone else be?

- Anxiety and terror: a child that has not experienced security finds it difficult to recreate it as an adult.

- Shame, guilt, self-hatred: if my parent did not take

care of me, or if I was deemed unworthy of love or care, that must mean I am bad.

- Cognitive distortions, dissociation, hallucinations: reality is too painful for me to see, so I create my own reality.

- Depression, passivity: what is the point in trying when I have felt so powerless as a child.

- Disturbed relatedness/detachment, numbing or withdrawal: I never experienced connection; I don't know how to. I feel lonely.

- Sexual promiscuity or aversion to sex, drug and alcohol abuse, eating disorders, suicide, self-mutilation, alienation from their bodies: I cannot feel my body; my body is not a safe place for me to be in. I use escapes to relieve this numbness or to numb down when the feelings are too intense.

- Anger and aggressive behavior: I feel powerless.

- Perfectionism, hyper-vigilance: maybe if I control everything, I will be safe.

- Questioning their sexuality and/or sexual orientation: I don't know who I am.

- Flashbacks: like PTSD, the traumatic memories are not stored as memories but are lived over and over every day. It is important to know that some of those flashbacks are experienced as a body sensation rather than an explicit memory.

Although I have learned to wear my BPD badge pride, to say I have lived with something that has terrori. me for years, and managed to come out on the other end, hair wild, eyes crazy yet beaming to be able to coexist with it, I find the name, at best, ironic and at worst, damaging.

The first irony is that the term "personality disorder" is saying that something is wrong with my personality, not my past. Our extreme fear comes from a childhood understanding that was underdeveloped at the time. This limited understanding turned the trauma, neglect (or perception of neglect) into feelings of shame and inadequacy. Do we really now want to categorise it as a personality disorder and add to that undeserved shame?

The second irony is that the term borderline was at some point coined as a middle ground between severe mental illness and health. How ironic is it that the group of black-and-white thinkers (thinking in absolutes, all of nothing) are diagnosed with being in the grey area between illness and health.

The third is that borderline is the line between neurosis and psychosis; it doesn't belong anywhere. How ironic is it that people who are worried about abandonment, being alone, and not belonging don't belong anywhere.

The name isn't exactly charming. It carries with it the negative connotation that borderlines choose to behave, feel and live in certain ways. I know everyone with any illness would pray, "Please, God, not this, give me anything else". And this is also true for the borderline.

Borderlines are viewed by therapists as difficult, slow, boring, overbearing, and downright draining cases to work with. Many therapists don't like working with the borderline because it is wildly misunderstood. The way I see it is a person with a borderline personality disorder, when triggered, is a child that feels very scared, very insecure and in desperate need of validation, love and security. What is not to love?

Being diagnosed as borderline is not easy either. If you look at the literature out there, much of it is laced with judgement, resistance and discrimination. Although some of us, myself included, feel a relief when diagnosed because it helps us understand and deal with the symptoms, many feel even more shame. Turning the diagnosis into another reason to blame ourselves or feel self-loathing is a habit that comes innately to the borderline even more intensely.

The most healing interactions I have had were of people who saw the terror that borderline has brought into my experiences and loved me anyway. To be held, seen, acknowledged, validated without the need to fix or correct me has brought about the most change. I truly believe that we have a long way to go with this diagnosis. And I believe that starting with the name might help. If the name stated the cause "childhood developmental trauma", how do you think that would change the way we look at the borderline? How would the blame be shifted? How would the stigmatisation be transformed? How would the shame shrink?

The stigmatisation needs to be ended first by the therapists and the educators. A friend of mine rushed a family member to the ER after a suicide attempt. He was seen by a psychiatrist who pulled my friend aside and said, "He is borderline. He is manipulating you; do not buy into his threats of suicide. He will do anything to get what he wants from you". My friend was mortified. Even if this was true, all it took was one successful attempt to lose this family member to a terrible accidental suicide.

Being borderline affects your relationships both with yourself and others. The discrimination against this diagnosis can be coming from imagining the interactions with the borderline. What I would love to say, on behalf of the borderlines that would let me, is that our intentions are not malicious. Our actions are driven by debilitating fear that sometimes makes us manipulative without intending to be so. That the destruction of our relationships is the last thing we want to do, yet we find ourselves doing it anyway. That the pain that you might be getting from us is a spillover from the pain that we live in every day.

Not knowing who we are also affects our relationships. There had been so many versions of me over the years that I can hardly connect to some versions of me. It feels like I have lived many lives, in many bodies, have loved many and lost many. I remember weeping after reading Memoirs of a Geisha because I identified so much with it. This happened often with books, movies and friends I interacted with. I felt like a chameleon for years, adapting my colour to my environment, not truly knowing who I was.

My black-and-white thinking tries to help me by compartmentalising those different version of me. I would label a version "good" or "bad", "strong" or "weak" to easily decide what parts of me to accept and which to outcast. I labelled my powerless childhood self as "weak", which caused much of the dissociation I lived with. It took real effort, and it still does, to consolidate all those versions of me into one whole.

The black-and-white thinking means that we will idealise you, see you as this perfect creature one moment, then hate you and want to push you away the next. It's not because we don't care; it's because we care too much. We care so much that not knowing exactly who you are and what you're capable of making us feel makes us so scared that we try to box you into the black and white of being a sinner or saint.

You don't have to try hard to hurt us; our skin is thin. I read once that being borderline is very much like not having skin, or having an exposed tooth nerve. Everything is heightened. We go on the highest highs and hit the lowest lows a few times within a single day sometimes. The ground doesn't feel stable beneath us; the world feels like a big scary place that is unpredictable and threatening.

Our fear of abandonment means that can we be overbearing at times, demanding closeness in a way that might feel suffocating, while at other times we will push you, sabotage our relationship and run away in an attempt to subconsciously prove that we were right all along, no one who gets to really know us stays around.

We feel empty, so we overwork ourselves, get involved in too many projects, form too many friendships or try to be too many things at once. Sometimes, this emptiness drives us into impulsive behaviour, food disorders, substance abuse, overspending, risk-taking and self-damage. What I have found is that the more I love myself, the better my coping mechanisms become. Over the years, I have replaced cutting myself with sports, distracting myself with napping and shopping with meditating.

When you are borderline, it is very difficult to calm yourself. Emotional deregulation means that self-soothing, although not impossible, takes practice to achieve. The borderline frantically looks for soothing from another person, rages in frustration or turns towards self-harm (through cutting, starving, binging, substance abuse and self-destruction). Or the opposite happens, withdrawing, feeling numb or isolating. Emotional deregulation can also cause episodes of mania (elated feelings and being overly energetic) or even hallucinations (visual or auditory).

What's interesting is that many view self-harm as a problem with the borderline, but it is actually a solution. Self-harm is the borderline's way of self-soothing; the real problem is the inability to self-soothe using healthy coping.

Understanding those symptoms made it easier for me to differentiate "this is me" vs "this is my borderline". Getting diagnosed meant that I knew what seeing the world from the lens of borderline is. I could therefore question my thoughts, the stories I told myself and how I behaved in the areas in which the borderline symptoms typically appear. This was disorienting at first. It felt like I did not know what was real anymore. What was accurate understanding and what was clouded by borderline? It is easy to also fall into shame in the beginning. When you realise that your disorder has caused you to live a lie, it becomes tricky to separate the responsibility you feel towards your recovery from the blame you have towards yourself about your past.

As the title of the book implies, I will be focusing in this book on finding balanced thinking as I believe that this is key for the borderline recovery. Whilst I will be sharing different practices and experiences that I found beneficial (and others that failed miserably), the eye of the hurricane to me will continue to be grey thinking and how to achieve it in different facets of the borderline life.

> "The diagnosis Borderline Personality Disorder (BPD) strikes fear and loathing in the hearts of most mental health providers. It is unquestionably one of the most stigmatizing and overused diagnoses in existence. Often diagnosing someone with this label is a clinical punch in the gut to the client and also a means of communicating warning to other clinicians. It is the 21st century version of the scarlet letter."
>
> – Jacqueline Simon Gunn

3 Grief

My first experience of the pain of being completely alone came when I was in high school. My therapist taught me to tell a story with the right amount of detail for maximum healing. So here it is:

I met my childhood best friend when I was seven. We hit it off almost immediately. She was a quiet, shy, beautiful girl with great big eyes, striking eyebrows, soft black hair and a soft smile. She let me take centre stage, and that suited me nicely. She let very few people in, and she let me in the most, and I was just fine with that. We spent summers together, the way teenagers dream of. We were so immersed in our summer-long goof arounds that we hardly noticed anyone but each other. We did nothing and had a blast. She waxed my legs the first time I had them waxed. Friends came and went, but we stayed the same. My friendship with her was the epitome of a stable, loving, secure and consistent friendship. She wasn't going anywhere; I wasn't going anywhere. We were good.

Fast forward ten years, on our last year of high school, her face suddenly swelled up. Her neck swelled up. It was so swollen it looked unreal, photoshopped. She was admitted into hospital a few days later, a biopsy was taken, and then came the news. My mother walked into my room, grave look on her face, and broke the news.

My best friend had cancer.

I spent every moment I could with her. We became closer in those last few months than we had in the ten years that we were friends. I was her support system. I was the only friend that had access to her when her immune system gave in. I felt closer to her than I ever had. We still did what teenage girls do; she still gushed over my outfits and wanted to be goofy. Then she got worse. No one could help her locally anymore. She had to be taken abroad to get her treatments. What was supposed to be a see you later turned into a goodbye. I never saw her again.

I can't remember our goodbye. What did I see the last time I looked at her? Did I not look long enough, or hard enough? Did I take that moment for granted? I resented that version of me for a very long time. That version of me that was sure that I would see her again. That optimistic version of me that thought bad things don't happen to good people. The part of me that had hope even after I was told that she had a very rare form of leukaemia.

I resented that naive version of me. The version that could not imagine that I would miss the last phone call she would make to me. That hopeful, bubbly, version of me that could not fathom the idea that I could lose her, that I would be wailing in her funeral "I lost my other half", that I would spend months by her mother's side just to feel her close, that

I would fall in love and marry her brother for the same reason, that I would birth her niece, seven years later, and she wouldn't be there to see it.

And it was the big one, the big loss that broke me. The grief that drowned me. Losing her was unfathomable. My eyes still tear up when I think of the way my heart broke over her, when I imagine her suffering in those last months. But what destroyed me was the loneliness I felt in my grief. My parents were beyond worried about me. I felt too big of a burden for my family. My teenage friends felt like they disappeared from around me. My worst nightmare had come true: I was alone.

I desperately wanted my friends to help me get through it. I wished my parents cared a little less so that I could dump my pain on them. Everything around me confirmed: you can't depend on anyone; you have to do this on your own.

That desperate need for someone to help me self-soothe and not having it was my earliest memory of what I would understand as borderline almost twenty years later. I wanted to feel safe, but because I didn't, I hated everyone I thought should have made me feel safe and didn't. I learned to poke a little for safety then run a thousand miles in the opposite direction if I did not get it exactly the way I wanted it. The borderline mantra of "I hate you, please don't leave me" had begun.

The fact that I was not soothed the way I wanted to hardened me. I remember thinking to myself at some point: "I am now strong. Nothing will break me". I thought that my refusal to feel difficult feelings was strength. I thought that shutting down my emotions like a switch was a superpower. I thought that being tough made me special.

That hardening came in the form of looking down on any sign of neediness, vulnerability or overwhelming sadness. For the rest of my teens and most of my twenties, I avoided funerals, the news, sad topics and the sound of wails. I rejected those qualities within other people, and I certainly rejected them within myself.

This was driven by the black-and-white thinking of borderline. Because being hopeful, vulnerable, close, attached caused so much pain in the past, I decided to do the extreme opposite. That was an attempt to protect me from pain, not considering the consequences of going to the other extreme. Like almost all extreme things, that plan did not work.

It takes a lot of effort to remain hard. And it definitely took a toll on me. This was when I turned to spirituality. When I started meditating, I burst into uncontrollable sobs many times. Sometimes, I knew what I was crying about, while at other times, tears came as a raw release of emotions that had no chance to express themselves, no place to explode out of. Meditating felt difficult in the beginning at times, to the point where I quit meditating a few times before I found the consistent practice that I still carry on today.

Yoga also caught me by surprise. When I started practising with my teacher, more often than not, it felt as if my body was weeping. I felt shame, vulnerability, loss, disorientation. Sometimes, I knew the narrative behind those feelings, and other times, the feeling came up with no background story. I was slowly opening up to the idea of owning my feelings and processing them rather than avoiding and pushing them down.

Meditation and Yoga made it safe for me to go back within myself. It provided glimpses of reality that had been severely fogged by the dark mist of anxiety, depression and trauma that I saw the world through.

It took me years to understand that only a brave heart can weep. And a braver heart to be seen weeping. That to grief is to mean that you have loved. Teaching Yoga was a great teacher of this lesson. Seeing my students becoming emotional, crying, grieving on their Yoga mats showed me how much strength and bravery it takes to be open, vulnerable, to allow feelings to come. I almost always did a little dance in my head when I saw it happen. I was excited for them to be looking into the dark parts within themselves; I knew that transformation was well on the way.

It took becoming a psychotherapist to understand that grief is not an emotion that needs to be corrected. That asking "What was she like?" is more useful than asking "How did she die?" That saying "That sounds really painful" is kinder than "You'll be okay". And that sometimes, holding someone's hand, and saying nothing at all, is the greatest gift you can give someone. It also taught me that the stages of grief are not linear; they come and go as they please. That even after twenty years of losing your best friend, you can still live in denial, having dreams that her death was a nightmare and that she was just hiding but that she is now back.

And I learned that no matter how much you think you have got your shit together, sometimes you don't. When someone I loved, almost two decades later, found an undiagnosed mass, I broke down. In my head, even before we receive an official diagnosis, it meant loss, grief and intolerable pain. I immediately went into worst-case scenario. Luckily, I had a therapy session on that same day.

My therapist helped me understand that in order to protect myself from my hopeful self, the self that I blamed for the pain I felt when I lost my best friend, I suppressed my hopeful self. My protection mechanism in what I saw as a high-stress situation, the possibility of loss, was to go into black-and-white thinking. It took conscious effort to imagine the grey: that there was a chance that mass was benign, that even if that mass was malignant, treatment and recovery was a possibility.

The difference between being hard then and being hard now is that I can now choose to be hard in some situations and not others. That it is now a conscious choice rather than a reactive reflex jerk because I can't handle the alternative.

Let me explain what I mean. In 2021, both my parents caught Covid-19. That, to me, was a nightmare come true. For fourteen months, I restricted my visits to them to good weather months where I could socially distance from them, outdoors, with a mask on. I had denied myself the joy of their company and my mother's very delicious food because I was worried I would make them sick. I could not live with the possibility of my parents catching it, let alone be the cause of it. When they mysteriously caught it, my world collapsed. Yet, it was important for me to temporarily remain solid, to detach my feelings, put them on the shelf for a little while, to make sure they receive the best possible medical care and deal with this crisis. I "stayed strong" because I wanted to make sure my sisters were OK. I "held it together" for a few days, and when they finally were stable, I let the tears come.

I knew that the fear of losing them was a normal feeling. I knew it meant that I loved my parents, that I was attached to them, that I wanted what was best for them. That those feelings of powerlessness weren't particularly nice.

Consciously deciding to postpone my feelings, knowing very well that I was doing so, felt very different than avoiding them. I felt I had the power, the choice, the wisdom to choose the best course of action in that situation. There wasn't a part of me that was rejecting the fear, the sadness, the frustration. I knew that I would get to that when the time was right. It felt kind, the way I responded to myself with "It's OK if you want to cry, we can do that a little later" instead of "There's no time to cry, you should be strong".

Here's the grey that I learned when it comes to grief:

Grief sucks. It is also necessary. Grief is not to be feared; it is the answer to unfathomable pain. It happens to everyone. The best journeys in grief are the ones that are not taken alone. That even in the pain of grief, meaning is possible.

Some people are good at being there for people who are grieving. Other people, despite good intentions, cannot do that. It is not because they want to abandon you/me, but rather because they might be scared of their own grief.

> "Grief, I've learned, is really just love. It's all the love you want to give, but cannot. All that unspent love gathers up in the corners of your eyes, the lump in your throat, and in that hollow part of your chest. Grief is just love with no place to go."
>
> – Jamie Anderson

4 Religion

My relationship with God started at a young age. I remember sitting and thinking, "Why are we here?" and then the answer came, "To connect with God", then another question, "But where were we before we were here?" and the answer came, "With God". And another, "But if we're not here, where would we be?", "Is there anyone that is not here?", "What if there was no here?" and "Is here even real?" And so those questions kept rolling until I felt transported out of this world, and my mind would reach its edge, and go tzzzap! Back into a three-dimensional world that seemed boring and dull.

I started praying when I was seven, five times a day without fail. I would have loved to say that the act of praying brought me connection to God, but it didn't. My connection with God wasn't around the praying; it was deeper than that. I remember doing it so fast that my parents giggled. I would be so busy playing all day and only remembered to pray when I heard the muezzin (caller for prayers) coughing into the microphone of the mosque next to my childhood home. At that point, I would remember the previous prayer and run to get it done quickly before I heard him call out "Allahu Akbar".

I was curious about religion, and I took in everything I learned at school seriously. I read on many topics outside of school and can argue different sharia (Islamic regulation) topics like a pro. Having that level of intellectual understanding at a young age added to the black-and-white thinking. I lacked the maturity then, borderline or not, to understand the spectrum of the human condition. To imagine, feel and connect to the many circumstances, conditioning and individual needs that fall outside of the rigid boxing of religious rules.

With time, God became more and more of an angry, judgemental, unknown, disconnected entity that sat in the sky, waiting for me to screw up to bestow terrible punishment on me. So when I became a teenager and started making less innocent mistakes, I felt more and more disconnected from God the more I learned from mainstream religious texts.

The straw was when I lost my best friend. The "bargaining" phase of my grief came in the form of I will hang on to God to make this alright . Subconsciously, I thought, maybe if I was a better person, such a terrible thing would not have happened to me. Feeling abandoned by everyone I wished was there for me (in exactly the way I needed them to be), I turned to God. I carried my Quraan with me everywhere I went, even the schoolyard. I wore a hijab (head cover) for a month. I buried myself in school work and did my best at being a "good girl".

I was in a lot of pain. That time of my life was synchronised with a typical time for borderline symptoms to appear. I felt terribly alone. Denial turned into anger. I felt angry towards God for taking my best friend away. And with puberty taking over, I felt angry that He had put instincts in me and then labelled them bad. I felt worthless, judged, and not good enough for Him. Those feelings kept growing, and God wasn't someone I could turn to anymore. I felt that God had abandoned me, forsaken me, forgotten all about me. At some point during my early twenties, I gave up completely on God. I thought, "Well, if I'm not good enough for You, then You are not good enough for me either".

Having lost the only source of consistent security in my life, my world fell apart even further. Having a relationship with God had given me the kind of security I craved as a borderline, although that is not unique to the borderline. God is omnipresent, omnipotent and omniscient. This means that God is everywhere, always present. God is strong, giving me security and safety. And God knows everything, so even when things aren't the way I want them to be, God knows better.

Having a best friend like that on your side, it's quite the loss when He is no longer participating. In those dark years, I attempted suicide the first time. There was nowhere left to go, nothing left to do; it was time to give up.

I was on a cocktail of drugs given to me by the second psychiatrist I was seeing. I was on anti-depressants, mood stabilisers and tranquillisers. Ironically, the tranquillisers had the side effect of inducing suicidal thoughts, although I'm not sure I could give them full credit. They felt good. Not the normal good, the good comparative to being severely depressed. They numbed me, made me care less, feel less sensitive. So one day, after feeling particularly fragile, right in the office I was working in, I took twelve times the dose I was prescribed. I drove home, high, and waited to die.

For those who never contemplated suicide seriously, let me tell you this much: When you decide to die, it is not because you want to be happy, it's because you want to stop being so sad. It is not the desire for a certain outcome that drives it, it is the desire away from suffering that does. It is not a cowardly choice, it takes a lot of courage to go against your own instinct to live. But when a person is suicidal, suicide is probably one of the very few things that provide a sense of power and choice. Do we think about our loved ones when we are that close to ending our lives? Well, I tried not to. To think I was leaving a child, a mother, a father, a family, a husband, and many friends behind would have been a hurdle I did not have the energy to jump over. Being impulsive helped. I took the pills, slowly, one by one, and waited.

I was lucky. I was divinely lucky that the tranquillisers I took to end my life knocked me into long sleep before I could carry on with another dose lethal enough to stop my heart. Looking back, I am also so very lucky to have endured such sadness. I am lucky that the state of my internal being was so bad that I had to end my life because only past my limits that left me broke–or broken-open rather–was I able to be born again.

I was also lucky that I found my relationship back to God through spirituality (more on that in the spirituality chapter). My approach to my relationship to God had completely changed. I stopped thinking of God as separate from me or working against me. God to me is now a friend, a mother, a father, a presence that holds my hand, wipes my tears and keeps me company. The consistency and resilience of my relationship with God remains unmatched. It is completely dependant on *my* openness to this relationship, not God's. At some point, I was not open to that relationship. I was angry even with God. But I am now.

I love God; I'm not God-fearing. I found that loving God brought me closer to God. Believing in a God that is uniquely mine, a God that just gets it, gets my limitations, my shit, my baggage and really has my back feels so much better. To be able to truly live that truth has saved my life.

Here's my grey when it comes to religion:

I love this story from the Kung Fu re-runs. Grasshopper, as a young boy, is standing by the pond, watching fish swimming. His master asks, "How many fish are there?"

"Twelve, Master," Grasshopper says.

"Good, and how many ponds are there?" Master asks.

Grasshopper looks confused. "One, Master."

"No, there are twelve ponds; twelve fish, twelve ponds."

The qualities of God that are seen depends on who is looking. A person's experience of God is as unique as the person himself. Our relationship with God is about experiencing God beyond concepts, religions, practices, workshops, books, rituals and ceremony. God is timeless and had always existed; this means that no monopoly of God can be claimed by any one path to truth. No one can claim that there is one way only to finding yourself or God because no one way worked for everyone every single time consistently. So even if you had no more offerings to give, no more mantras to chant, no more verses to recite, no more prayers to say, no more meditations to sit, no more seva (selfless charity) to serve, no more books to read, no more alms to give, no more feelings to release, no more malas (prayer beads) to count, bowing, incense, or even effort to offer, you could still find yourself and find God.

Our relationship with God can be tailored to the individual rather than tailor the individual to the relationship. I don't believe religion was given for us to have rules. Nor do I believe that the purpose of religion is for us to judge ourselves (or others) harshly or to hold grudges. Religions are merely guidelines that help us to move away from complicating our lives. They are about how we feel about ourselves and the world around us. It's supposed to make us feel good about ourselves and the world, although that is not always an experience of pleasure.

A simple way I gauge my religious beliefs now is: Does this make me feel closer or further from God? Does this help me do better or worse? Does this make me feel more connected to other people or disconnected from them? Answering those questions honestly regardless of what I believe and re-examining my beliefs often helps me keep track of what helps me get closer to God and what doesn't.

My approach to my relationship with God is fluid, to say the least. I have prayed in churches, called out Allah in Hindu temples and meditated in the Ka'abah. I have found

God in deep grief and singing children. God comes in no form and in all forms. He's within me and without me. He is a She, and She is a He, and it won't matter one bit because I carry Him/Her in my heart.

> "God almighty says: I am as my slave thinks, and I am with him when he remembers me. If he calls me within him Self, I call him within my Self. And if he remembers me in a good crowd, I remember him in a better crowd." – Mohammed PBUH

5 Spirituality

Spirituality has played a major role in my recovery. In this chapter, I dive into the spiritual practices that have helped me along the way. I talk about what worked for me and what didn't and what I think went right/wrong. I also share things that I have learned from those practices. What is worth noting though is, this chapter is worthless if you do not practice what you learn. To know something in your mind and to have experienced it, lived it and embodied it does not give the same result. It is vital that you find your own practice and experiences. Nothing you will read here will change your life unless you take this map, get up, and go somewhere.

Meditation/Energy Healing

I have grouped meditation with healing energy as my own experience with those two things has been intertwined. I met my wonderful Reiki teacher, Master Fawzia Alsindi, back in 2009. Little did I know that this woman would save my life.

I went into her class with the intention of proving that what she was doing was hocus-pocus. Yet, a part of me was hoping that something would save me from the incredible pain I was in. Another part of me was resigned, sceptical and cynical.

I walked into her Reiki course at a very low point in my life. I had been diagnosed with depression, bipolar and was actively suicidal (more on this in the therapy chapter). This was a final, half-assed attempt to save my own life, a hail Mary if you like. I felt helpless, worthless, lost and stuck. I was leading a life in which I did not recognise myself anymore (can you say Borderline?). I was in despair, and I saw no hope. I had tried antidepressants and gone off them. I wanted something to work, but I didn't think anything could.

Master Fawzia's unconditional acceptance, love and limitless wisdom were key in my ability to relax into the guided meditations she offered. I believe she initially provided the safety I needed to go within myself.

My first few experiences of meditation were intense. The meditation practices provided the space I needed from my mind. It gave me a break of silence from that constant terror that was happening in my head. It was a helicopter view of the landscape of my mind. I fell in love with it almost immediately. I craved the breaks from my mind, and so it was easy to commit to a consistent practice. Meditation gave me something to do. It gave me not only a distraction but also the superpower of not feeling severely uncomfortable constantly.

This was one of the few times that black-and-white thinking helped. I committed to meditating a minimum of an hour a day; this went on for months. Although my first few experiences were pleasant, many that followed weren't. Master Fawzia warned us that the healing process would not be an easy one. She also taught us to rejoice when the tears came, that it meant healing and shedding old wounds.

Meditation was the first and only way I knew to self-soothe. My fellow borderlines will understand how priceless this is. The ability to make ourselves feel better is not something we can do, not without training. My head felt like there was a bully that lived inside of it; now, I could shut this bully up, even if that silence was temporary.

Meditation ruined me. The rush I got from shopping, overexerting myself socially and seeking highs gradually subsided. The sweetness I got from connecting to the deepest, quietest, most peaceful parts of myself remains unmatched (maybe with the exception of getting hugs from my daughter).

If you are thinking that meditation is for the calm/introverted types, then I want to iterate here that I am an extreme extrovert. Until I was seventeen and went to university, I hardly had any alone time (at which point I had a major meltdown, but that's another story). I did not like being alone with myself. My thoughts were too loud. Silence was uncomfortable. I am hyper, easily distracted and hate small details. I didn't like me; why would I want to be left alone with me?

Meditation is my safe place. Going within feels soothing, calming. I have a romantic, loving relationship with myself (although, like all romantic relationships, it has its ups and downs). But meditation taught me that I'm alright. I'm cool. I'm okay. I can hang out with me. Hanging out with myself in meditation really acts like a recharge button. It's my mini-vacation that I can take for free, anytime, anywhere. This ability to hang out with myself took a lot of pressure off of my relationships with others and my expectations of them. I can hold the space for myself; I do not always need someone else to do it for me anymore.

I found that it doesn't matter what technique you use to meditate, so long you stick to it. An average of three months, three to five times a week, with the same technique will give you the best results. Build up to a minimum of twenty minutes per sit. I also find it doesn't matter if you're sitting cross-legged or on a chair; the less complaints from the body, the better. I would highly suggest not lying down, though; you might fall asleep, and while sleep is good for you, it does not do what meditation does. Here are a few of the techniques I love:

- **Spinal breathing**: sitting comfortably, bring your awareness to your tailbone. As you inhale, imagine a thread of light rising from your tailbone until you reach with your awareness your third eye, the space between your eyebrows. As you exhale, imagine this thread of light moving back down to your tailbone. You might find that some areas feel "stuck". If that happens, simply go around whatever obstacle you face, take the easiest path.

- **Metta meditation**: loving-kindness meditation works wonders for the borderline as it addresses our relationships with ourselves and with others. Sitting comfortably, see yourself, or feel yourself. Feel what it's like to be you. Imagine love radiating out of your own heart to yourself. If you struggle with this in the beginning, find one quality that you like about yourself and use that as a reason to love yourself. If you still find that difficult, imagine yourself as a baby or a toddler. Repeat in your heart, "May I be happy, may I be healthy, may I be free". Next, imagine someone you find very easy to love, radiate the same loving kindness from your heart towards him/her/them. "May he/she/they be happy, may he/she/they be healthy, may he/she/they be free". Then, find someone you have been in conflict with, consider what it is like to be them for a few moments, knowing that just like you, they wish to be happy, and radiate your loving-kindness towards them. "May he/she/they be happy, may he/she/they be healthy, may he/she/they be free". Next, expand your awareness to your country, then other countries, the planet, then the entire universe, repeating the same prayer. End by imagining all the love that you radiated out coming back to you, knowing that you are worthy and deserving of all this love.

What I want to point out here is a trap that I fell into with this meditation. Just because you feel loving-kindness towards someone who has hurt you does not mean you have to act on it. Meditation has taught me to self-soothe; I hope it teaches you that too. If you jump from meditating to trying to soothe yourself by getting someone else to engage with you, then you're missing out on a chance to learn how to do that for yourself. There will be times where reconciliation will happen. My experience has taught me that reconciling works best after you have taken care of your emotions internally.

- **Mindfulness meditation**: sitting comfortably, focus on the air coming in and out of your body. You will find that within seconds, your mind will wander off into another topic. As soon as you're aware that it has, come back to the breath. Do this over and over again. Do not get involved with your mind, do not entertain it, and do not fight it; just let it run in the background. What will begin to happen with time is that while your mind will demand your attention, you will have the choice, the wisdom and the power to either give your attention or not. This is a skill that will spill over into your life too. The way I like to explain this is: imagine if you were sitting with your best friend, and there was a movie playing. Your breath is your best friend; the movie is the chatter in your mind. If you are more interested in the movie (which is how it is in the beginning), you lose a chance to bond with your best friend. After some time, you will alternate between watching the movie and engaging with your best friend. After some practice, you will be completely immersed in conversation with your best friend. And while the movie might be running in the background, you will just let it run, seeing it as a badly produced, uninteresting background noise while your real interest is in your best friend.

This reminds me of a story told by my dear yoga philosophy teacher, Rose Baudin. Rose was doing a Vipassana retreat. This is a course of ten days of silence with long hours of meditation where aspirants seek the truth by stilling the mind through meditation and going within. There is no talking, physical activity (except light walking), reading, writing or even eye contact. However, retreaters are given the chance to speak with one of the teachers that run the retreat at regular intervals to make sure that their practice is effective.

As Rose was waiting for her turn to speak to her teacher, she heard the person in front of her tell the teacher the story of how her meditation went that morning. She said: "I had such a powerful meditation, I saw all the people I had wronged, and I apologised to them, I cried, and I regret all the wrongs I had done. I held them in my arms, and they completely forgave me. I then saw all the people that had wronged me, and one by one, I held them and forgave them. I feel very light, and I am so glad that I am able to release such emotions".

While the lady was telling her story, the teacher had a very neutral look on her face. Rose, on the other hand, being the compassionate being that she is, really felt for this person, began to feel emotional but also thought, "Oh my, I haven't had any of those experiences this lady is talking about. I wonder if my meditation was any good".

And at that moment, the teacher looked at this lady straight in the eye and said, "Do not engage with content".

I use this story every time I teach meditation. The mind will dress up as many characters in an attempt to grab your attention. The mind is doing its job correctly. Your job is not to always give your attention. If you do not associate so strongly with the content of your thoughts, then thoughts would not have such a strong grip on you. You would then allow thoughts to come and go and easily be able to filter through them. They would then become a "temporary inconvenience", as the great Zen master Mooji describes them. Mooji says that no one is exempt from the rising of those self-centred thoughts, the "I-attacks" as he calls them, but that "a sign of that deeper maturity that you can let anything come, any visitor can come, but they can't stay...Anybody can come, but no sleepovers". This tells you that it is natural and non-problematic for the mind to generate thoughts. But thoughts lose their power very quickly if we turn our attention away from them and back into something present and neutral such as the breath.

There are endless lessons that came from my meditation practice. I share a few of them below. As I said before, none of those lessons will count if you do not experience them for yourself. Some of those might come up for you too, and some might not, while other lessons unique to you might come up.

1. Let it Go: I don't say this in an avoidant "good vibes only" way. I'm saying that my ability to let things slide when I choose to was born because of

meditation. In the past, I would remain highly triggered for hours, days or even months without being able to come down. Learning to let it go means that I now can choose to sometimes turn my attention from one thing to something else. I have a choice on what to focus on and when. It's not a running away from uncomfortable feelings but rather hitting a stop button when I feel a thought has run its course and there is no point in dwelling in it longer. Meditation is a direct practice of letting go that cannot be done intellectually by force.

2. Surrender: I speak about surrender at length in the surrender chapter. Meditation was a vital practice for surrender. Surrender meant that I have trust, safety and meaning even when things aren't going my way. When there is trust in my heart that things will turn out okay, the anxiety shrinks. When I remain non attached, life becomes more exciting and fulfilling; the possibilities are endless.

3. Pause: The mind always has a big flashy story to sell. Pausing makes me consider what will matter and what will not. If I choose to react, I can still do so after pausing. In conflict, the mind tries to justify, explain, attack and defend. There had been very few instances in my life where this had been effective. Similar to letting go, pausing is a conscious allowing of time and space that I gift myself to process, cool down and skilfully find a win-win situation where possible.

4. Connection: This will sound so cheesy, but We Are One. There is no win-lose situation; it is either win-win or lose-lose. Even if making someone (including yourself) feel bad temporarily feels good, it will feel bad in the long run. We rise by raising each other up. Being kind feels good. Loving someone else feels good. This is because kindness and love are natural to us. This is not always possible, but in the instances where it is, it's a better option.

5. You are not your mind: I can say this till I turn blue in the face, but until you experience the space between you and your mind, it will not make any sense. An untrained mind will continue to terrorise you like a bully's voice that permanently lives within your head. Not everything your mind says is true, accurate, necessary or helpful. But I found that in order to examine thoughts, you need the space from them. Meditation helps you do that by practising separating yourself from that voice. The way I teach it is going through life is like driving a car; you have to keep your eyes on the road. The road is the present moment: the breath, the way your body feels, what is happening right now. In the meantime, the mind acts like the attention-seeking child in the back seat. This child is needy, insecure, loud and demanding. The demands of this child are not the problem; our reaction to them is. If we continue to give in to the demands of this child, it will grow stronger and more creative in the ways it gets you to slave for its needs. But if you keep calm, keep your eyes on the road and

watch it with amusement rather than resistance, it is more likely to calm down or give up long enough to give you peaceful moments of silence.

6. Relationships Count: No matter how strong, independent or spiritual you get, you *need* people. We are social beings at a cellular level. You need people to help you out when you cannot help yourself. You also need to feel deep connections of love and care, especially when you struggle to love yourself. But you also need people to challenge you. People that trigger you are your teachers; they show you the blind spots of where the work needs to be done. All relationships, good or bad, can be used as a map of our inner world. Helping us explore and strengthen our understanding of ourselves, the world, and God. Recognising that the people in our lives can be great teachers of love, patience, tolerance and acceptance makes every interaction meaningful and an opportunity to grow: a blessing, or a blessing in disguise.

7. Focus on what matters: What's the big picture? What will matter in the end? What will I regret? Meditation helps me declutter things that will not matter in the end: our looks, maintaining meaningless habits and relationships, taking tasks that mean nothing to us and so on.

8. You do You: Meditation gave me the chance to get to know myself. By knowing myself, I rediscovered what I loved. Interestingly, by knowing myself, I also

saw that I was alright, and so I learned to love myself. This gave me permission to do things I love, have fun, express myself, take myself less seriously and just be who I want to be.

9. Love yourself: Again, a cliche catchphrase. But away from the take a bubble bath and get a massage thing (which is great sometimes), being an impulsive borderline meant that I was stuck in a cycle of impulsive behaviour, had regrets, hated myself, engaged in more impulsive behaviour. Meditating gave me the space to examine impulsive behaviours and set a standard of ethics that, very selfishly, makes me feel better about myself. Having ethics is about doing things that complicate my life the least. It's not a high horse; it's a clear understanding of the consequence of doing something regretful: regret and shame, oh debilitating, shackling shame.

10. Acceptance: Some things cannot change. The next best thing is to accept them. This applies to the past; being judgemental about mistakes I made in the past breeds self-loathing and shame that kept me stuck in an endless loop. It did not help me do better. I think a part of me held on to the shame because letting go of it meant letting myself off the hook, which is not the case. A lot of the pain I felt during depression and the main reason I tried to take my own life was that I could not accept myself or life as it was. What I learned is that change is launched by acceptance (which sounds like an oxymoron). Having a clear vision of where I want to go in life started with a clear

acceptance of where I am now. This vision also has the flexibility, trust and wisdom to know that my plans, path and timelines can change into something completely different.

11. It's OK to change your mind: I love changing my mind; it's telling me I can think in the grey. I'm open to new ideas, new ways of thinking, new ways of being. It's telling me I'm all grown up, mature and wise, doing okay. I am constantly evolving. Dropping ideas, concepts and beliefs allows for growth and transformation. I have decided to free myself from attachment even to things I have learned, lived and believed in. Life will continue to teach me lessons that will sometimes be joyful and at other times painful. I will continue to listen to my heart, love myself and look for ways to connect with others in the process.

Meditation is a priceless practice of mindfulness, an essential tool for the recovery of the borderline. However, my experience was that meditation could be used as a tool for dissociation. Dissociation is not a bad idea when the torment of your mind has you at the edge of suicide. In fact, dissociation might save your life.

Meditation gave me wisdom, insight and perspective. If I could do it all over again, I would still meditate. I still meditate. I don't see a time in my life where I won't. I enjoy it, and it helps me, and it has helped millions of people, borderline or not. A fellow psychotherapist asked me once if I thought it was a good idea for a borderline to meditate since it's a form of dissociation, and my answer was, "Yes, because regular dissociation doesn't feel good after I come back, but meditation does". So here's my grey when it comes to meditation:

Meditation has exceptional potential at rewiring your mind. It gives the kind of experiential insight that can transform and heal. I understand it is not for everyone, especially the seated practice (which might be better to initially replace with moving meditation). But I stand by meditation for the borderline as the work of organising thoughts is a very difficult task without it. I don't believe meditation fixes everything. There are other practices that are vital for the recovery of the borderline, but meditation is hell of a start.

Yoga

Here's another cliche catchphrase: Yoga chose me. After the c-section I went through to deliver my daughter, Yoga was the only form of movement I could handle. I remember walking out of my first Yoga class in 2007 and calling all of my friends to tell them they were missing out.

Despite common belief, the purpose of Yoga is not a perfect handstand on the beach in a bikini (though that's a nice bonus). The Yoga Sutras, the vast collection of the original yoga guidelines, defines Yoga as:

"Yoga Chitta Vrtti Nirodhah"

This translates to: Yoga is the restraint of mental modifications or fluctuations of consciousness. In other words: Equanimity.

Equanimity is the cessation of internal conflict; it is

when all the parts of you are in agreement. Your body is clearly communicating to your mind which is collaboratively working with your heart which is strongly connected to your spirit. I love it when I set up my students by asking, "Why are you here in this yoga class?" and they respond, "To connect mind, body and spirit". Nice catchphrase. What does that mean? Have you felt your spirit? Have you met it? Have you experienced it? How can you connect it if you haven't? They walk right into that one.

And when I explain equanimity, they often follow up with another catchphrase that is overused and misunderstood: "It's all good". No, actually, it's all not good. In fact, most people who start Yoga (myself included) do so because it is not good at all. They show up on the mat in an attempt to fix everything that is not good.

Equanimity is being OK with things not being good; it is also being OK with things being good. You see, the trap is that the mind creates a lot of resistance to what *is*. When you don't have what you want, you're daydreaming of it, and when you have what you want, you're anxious about losing it. Eckhart Tolle says it beautifully, "The ego wants to want more than it wants to have".

Here's a classical example from my own life: I was in a long term, long distance relationship with my then finance for four years while I was abroad studying. During those four years at university, I only got to see my fiancé during Christmas, Easter and summer holidays. Every moment I lived was a longing to the moment we met again. Worse still, I lived for the moment where I would finally go back, get married and live with the love of my life.

The four years passed, painfully slowly but surely. I went back home, got married and left for my honeymoon. We arrived in Phuket, Thailand. It was my first experience of tropical weather and I was in love with it. The beauty of nature and the people overwhelmed me. We walked into our hotel room and it was the most beautiful hotel room I had ever been into, filled with the smell of lemongrass, a customized cake sat in the corner, it was perfect. The room had a massive balcony that overlooked the most stunning ocean I had ever seen. I stood in that balcony and realised that I had finally arrived to the moment I had been waiting for for four long years. I was breathless, then I sobbed. My then husband looked puzzled. I explained between sobs "I will never be this happy again".

You see, my journey towards my destination was miserable that my destination was miserable too. To think that taking a mind that was disturbed, anxious, attached and lacking into the perfect moment and expect it to be still, abundant and content was an impossible ask.

> "If you don't get what you want, you suffer, if you get what you don't want, you suffer, even when you get exactly what you want, you still suffer because you can't hold on to it forever."
>
> – Socrates

Yoga is a practice of both contentment and presence. It is not about seeking happiness or joy but rather a peaceful engagement in the present. It is the ability to observe both with equal compassion and peace the state of not having a preference. It is finding the strength to accept external circumstances regardless of what we have been taught to call them.

This state of "I don't mind", as Zen master Mooji describes it, does not mean that we don't care, it does not mean that we are not engaged with the world, nor does it mean that we are passive and withdrawn. On the contrary, equanimity is the active involvement with reality and with the Now. If we look at all our negative emotions, we will see that behind them, there is a thought that is not present, not in this moment. Many of our thoughts that create suffering are revolved around a regretful past or a fearful future.

My ex-husband found himself jobless at some point in our marriage. Our daughter was five and went to a very expensive school. We had a mortgage on the house, and I hardly earned a quarter of what he did. I was happy in that moment that years of practice paid off. Instead of my mind going, "He won't be able to get a job that pays this good"(thought in the future) or "How could they do this after all the hard work he put in? We should never have bought this house" (thought of the past), I found that I felt peaceful. Instead, my inner voice said, "Right now, we are living in a house, we are safe, there is food in the fridge. We are all healthy, and that is all that matters. The worst-case scenario is that we sell this house and start over, which is not the end of the world. We've done it before; we can do it again.

My husband has all the knowledge, ability and will to find another job". This might seem like a small achievement, but for a person with BPD, not falling into extreme anxiety is a rewarding milestone. Not falling into despair, depression or rage was not something that was available to me without this practice. Yoga taught me to be grounded in the present, which helped me remain equanimous and peaceful.

Equanimity is the ability to bring your attention completely to this moment. This ability to remain equanimous and present is portrayed in a beautiful Zen story:

There was a well-respected Zen master named Hakuin who lived in an honourable, peaceful and realized way. Near his house lived a beautiful Japanese girl. This girl, out of the blue, was found out to be pregnant. Needless to say, her parents were furious. After pressuring the girl to say the truth, she told her parents that the father was Master Hakuin. Her parents marched to Hakuin and gave him a piece of their mind. Upon listening to the accusations and insults, all he responded with was, "Is that so?"

They then told the whole village about how much of a fraud Hakuin was. The whole village asked Hakuin to leave, letting him know how unworthy he was of their respect and love. Hakuin became an outcast by the whole village. When the child was born, the parents took the baby to the master and demanded that he took care of her since he was the father. All Master Hakuin responded with was, "Is that so?" as he accepted the child.

A year later, the girl was overwhelmed with guilt and confessed to her parents that the father of the child was actually the young man who worked at the fish market. The family went back to Master Hakuin to apologize and ask for forgiveness. Their apology was elaborate and sincere. As Master Hakuin handed back the child, all he said was, "Is that so?"

I get it; it's a far stretch. But Yoga taught me that in many cases, remaining as an accepting, compassionate witness serves me best. Equanimity means that our discrimination towards the type of experiences, settings, life rules and preferences subside enough for us to observe the world as it is. When we stop labelling things as "good" or "bad", this opens up many doors and possibilities. Accepting things as they are means that the image that we hold in our heads about how the world should be becomes flexible. This can drastically reduce suffering. I often share the below paragraph with students:

> *"At the base of the conditioned mind is a wanting. This wanting takes many forms. It wants to be secure. It wants to be happy. It wants to survive. It wants to be loved. It also has specific wants: objects of desire, friendships, food, this color or that color, this kind of surrounding or some other kind. There's wanting not to have pain. There's wanting to be enlightened. There's wanting things to be as we wish they were. Our daydreams are imaginings of getting what we want; nightmares of being blocked from what we want. The planning mind tries to assure satisfaction. Most thought is based on the satisfaction of desires. Therefore, much thought has at its root a dissatisfaction with what is. Wanting is the*

> *urge for the next moment to contain what this moment does not. When there's wanting in the mind, that moment feels incomplete. Wanting is seeking elsewhere.*
>
> *Completeness is being right here."* – Stephen Levine, 1979

As I shared in meditation, here are the lessons I learned from practising Yoga that I hope you get to experience for yourself too:

- Mind over matter: imagining something happening in your body (like your head touching the floor in a forward fold) is very helpful in making it happen. We are often fixated on what we do not want. Having a clear image of what we do makes it easier to get there.

- Sometimes, doing less gets you there faster: Not all things in life require effort, determination and push.

- Some things in life require softness, allowing and surrender. Your muscles lengthen and stretch when you drop the control the most.

- Where your attention goes, energy flows: focusing your attention on the sensations in your body rather than distracting yourself from them will give you the best results. If the sensation is not safe[1], you can

---

[1] Safe sensations are stretching and strengthening. Unsafe sensations are injuries and injury causing as well as any traumatic sensations you are not ready to experience.

always move out of the pose. If it is safe, notice how you can work with it.

- Balance is a mirage: You can only dance around balance, you think you got it, but you are constantly fluctuating around it. The only thing you can do is remain present to return as close to it as you can as soon as you can. Try this: stand on one foot and notice how balance works.

- Your body remembers everything. There are things that your mind is incapable of processing, and it doesn't necessarily have to. Your memories are stored in your cells, and your body is a powerful vehicle that can help you release those memories.

- The narrative is not always important. Sometimes it is okay to feel sad, ashamed, angry, or even elated without knowing exactly why. An emotion can be experienced fully without the narrative.

- Just because something did not work the many times you tried it before doesn't mean it won't work today. Try again anyway, have fun trying.

- Just because something worked before doesn't mean it will continue to. Learn to adapt your practice and life to you rather than force yourself into a life (or pose) you no longer fit in.

- No two people are the same. There is beauty in the diversity of our abilities, strengths, restrictions, experiences. Trying to fit everyone into one box is to turn a rainbow into a colourless life.

- The only way out is through. There are no shortcuts, no magic pills, no one can do anything for you. You have to do it yourself. Others can support you, share their knowledge and experiences, but in the end, the work is on you. Having bravery to go into your wounds will free you from the fear of them surfacing.

- Important and serious are not the same thing. You can have fun and achieve great things. Seriousness can be unnecessary and wasted effort.

- Patience is key. Ambition can sometimes be the break in your progress. Steady, small doses of effort are a safer and more rewarding approach to your goals.

- Slower is more advanced: To move slowly, deliberately and mindfully in a world that is obsessed with achieving mass production and deadlines is rebellion. It takes more effort, focus and mastery to do something slowly and well.

- Relax into your effort: If you cannot relax, then you're doing too much. Try doing less, and test the relaxing there.

- Shoulders away from the ears: Notice where you hold tension in the body; even when you have very little choice in things that are happening around you, you have the choice to create the body language of relaxation and confidence.

- Being vulnerable is brave: trying something you

might fail at, exposing something you're trying to hide and softening where you are rigid takes bravery and courage.

- Be kind to yourself: only ask of yourself what is reasonable and possible. Listen carefully to how you speak to yourself; it matters.

- What's it like being you: no one in the entire universe is having the exact experience you're having in this moment. It would be a waste for you not to connect to it.

- What others can and can't do doesn't give to or take from your experience: Sure, you can be inspired by someone's ability to do something, but we all walk our paths individually, even when we witness each others' walking.

- Rest it not optional: consistency, continuity and resilience depend on your ability to rest. Rest is the harvest time where you integrate what you learn into your core, from which change and transformation are possible. Rest is the antidote to quitting.

- Keep your sense of humour: you will fall on your ass, and you won't look cool doing it. Remain humble, don't take yourself too seriously, and have fun in the process.

- It depends: This is my ultimate grey thinking win from teaching thousands of people Yoga in the last ten years. Regardless of the question (How often should I practice? How should my hips be aligned? Feet together or hip-width? Pelvis tilts forward or back? etc.), the answer is always: it depends. Yoga and life are not one size fit all. Everybody is different, and every body is different. Find the right answer for you now; if that answer changes later, then change it!

This is my grey when it comes to Yoga:

Yoga remains as one of the top therapies for trauma, which is essentially what borderline is. My personal experience with Yoga had been transformational even before I understood how or why it worked. It provided a platform for me to take ownership of my body back. It made it safe for me to live in my body. To live in an embodied way. It did not solve all my problems (nothing ever did), but it gave me an outlet and a space to process emotions that are difficult to process with words.

When I first became a Yoga teacher, my practice was very young. I was a sponge that took on every word that my teacher said. I had nothing else to reply on because I didn't have enough practice. I am eternally grateful for everything I learned. It provided me with such a strong foundation. My teachers' years of experience saved me from making terrible mistakes (most of the time, when I was listening anyway). It gave me great insight into what I loved to teach and how.

And years of practice and teaching taught me that there is more than one right answer (remember: it depends). It took maturity of understanding the practice to let go of rigid ideas beyond "right" and "wrong". Your thinking becomes flexible when it becomes so obvious that there is more than one right answer.

This was a big aha moment for me. It spilt over other areas in my life. Life is constantly evolving, so are we, so is our understanding of it. Something may be true to one person and not the other. It may be true in one moment and not the next. It may be true in one context and not the next.

Our Yoga practice changes through our lifetime as both our physical abilities and our mental and emotional needs change. Yoga does not need to take a specific form; there are so many schools of thought when it comes to yoga, and there is a flavour of it for everyone.

> "Yoga is concerned with freedom from suffering. The first step is to engage in introspection and thereby understand the inner obstacles that can be overcome. The purpose of yogic tools is to weaken the hindrances which obstruct freedom of the soul."
>
> – Patanjali

6 Mindfulness

The reasons I dive into mindfulness in this chapter are: One, it was a crucial part of my recovery, and I can only preach what I practised. Two, the borderline struggles to differentiate fact from feeling, mindfulness creates the practice needed for that distinction. Three, mindfulness ensured a smooth introduction into parts therapy (discussed in the therapy chapter); it made it easier for me to separate "me" from "my mind" and "my Soul" from "my Ego".

In order to explain mindfulness, I need to first define what the mind is, and what we are not.

What the mind is

The mind is the bird's eye from which we see the world. The human mind was designed with very specific functions and ways to work. It was not designed to be used all day, every day. According to an article published by the National Science Foundation in 2001, humans have an average of 12,000 to 60,000 thoughts a day, 95% of which are thoughts that we had the day before, and 80% are negative. In this day and age, human beings have been programmed to overuse their minds, leaving them ineffective, agitated and overstimulated. This has caused humans to suffer from what we can safely call the pandemic of our time: depression, anxiety and sleep problems.

The problem with the human mind is the way it is used (or misused rather). I met a beautiful Reiki master once who said to me, "If we used our arms the way we used our minds, we would be walking around waving our arms aimlessly all day".

The Yoga tradition helps us understand the way in which the mind works by explaining the four main players in it. If we imagine that our mind was a household, each one of those players will represent a character within that house.

a. Manas—The lower mind | Imagine this to be the Maid. She should not really have a say in any decision making within the house as this really should be done by the head of the household, say Mom. However, when untrained, she will try to make decisions. She is supposed to carry out the orders from Mom only, but she questions and doubts, which causes issues when excessive. If another member of the house speaks louder than Mom, she will take the orders from them instead. This is the lower mind through which this house interacts with the world. Manas will cause "Prajna Paradha", what is known in Ayurveda, the ancient reigning practice of medicine in India, as "crimes against wisdom".

b. Citta—The Storehouse of Memory | Imagine this to be the younger sister that remembers everything! She's like a complex library of memory, sensation and experiences. She is helpful when she reminds us not to touch fire because it had been hot before, for example, but she can cause difficulty if she does not coordinate with others. She will often shout things out to Manas, leaving Mom's voice unheard.

c. Ahamkara—The Ego | The loud, obnoxious teenage boy in the house. Everything he says is about "I" and "Mine". He feels separate, distinctive, important, different and special. He is also the main reason this household is separate from other households. Whenever Citta recalls a memory, he will go on about how he likes this and doesn't like that. How he demands this and refuses that. He says it with such a loud voice that Manas will take his orders.

d. Buddhi—Intuition (from the Sanskrit word "Budh", which means "awakened") | This is Mom. Mom was created to make all our decisions, but she is very soft-spoken. She will begin to speak louder the more we listen to her. This is our "gut feeling" or the "sound of the soul" or "our third eye". It does not always make logical sense, but it always knows what's in the best interest of everyone.

Let's say, for example, that you are trying to quit smoking. You would walk out of a business meeting and feel stressed. The conversation in your head will go something like this:

Citta (Sister): "Remember when you felt stressed a hundred times before and always reached for a cigarette?"

Here, Manas (Maid) is listening carefully for cues and orders.

Buddhi (Mom) [whispering]: "Don't even think about it; we're trying to quit."

If you do not listen immediately to the sound of Buddhi and act upon it, the other players in the mind will begin interfering with your decision-making.

Manas (Maid): "Really? But we did it so many times before!"

Ahamkara (Brother): "I really like to have a cigarette after a stressful situation, it always calms me down, I want a cigarette, I should have one, I do what I want."

Buddhi (Mom) [whispers]: "It's bad for you, don't do it."

Manas (Maid): "Let's go get a cigarette."

Buddhi is what is often referred to as intuition or gut feeling. This is the soft whisper that ignoring is often followed with regret "I knew I should have...". Yoga tells us that the more Buddhi is listened to, the louder and clearer it gets; this is how this voice is developed and strengthened. Listening to this voice takes practise; to be able to listen to it, personal preferences and desires need to be shelved momentarily. Logic also needs to be shelved because Buddhi is not always logical and so rationalising the sound of the gut does not always work. I have found that sometimes all I have to do is trust that things will become clearer later, even if they do not make sense right now.

Just like Buddhi has a strong role, so does Ahamkara (the Ego). The Ego is not our enemy; it is designed for our survival. Ahamkara's survival instincts are so strong they override logic and love. The Ego connects us to the physical reality in order to connect our inner world to our outer world. It is constantly looking out for threats (new people, unfamiliar settings, fear of rejection, etc.).

What is important for everyone, and the borderline in particular, is the distinction of those two sounds.

On the one hand, borderline causes the hyper-vigilance of seeing others as threat of abandonment and rejection. This is a thought of separation rather than connection, a distinct characteristic of the Ego.

On the other hand, borderline blurs the sense of Self, which is really the job of the Ego; this causes trouble with boundaries.

This internal battle of "I hate you, please don't leave me" can only be settled once those two parts of ourselves can be consolidated into one. A technique I use in the therapy room is to get those parts to talk, argue and debate until they come up with a common and agreeable solution for both parts.

On top of that, although we are told to "listen to our gut", sometimes the "gut" and the "mind" sound the same. It is sometimes difficult to differentiate between what is the choice of the soul, the heart, the universe and what is the choice of the ego, the mind, and fear.

I had met my spiritual teacher, a realised sage that teaches compassion and surrender in India, in 2014. My teacher is an embodiment of unconditional love, and she is therefore referred to by her students as "Amma", which translates in Indian to "Mother". When I asked Amma how can we tell the difference between the mind and the soul in the instances that they sound so alike, she said that the soul is always "sure". That there is no hesitation with the soul, it will speak clearly and with confidence, while the mind hesitates, questions and confuses.

So understanding those two parts of the mind and using them as the situation dictates is crucial for the borderline. The Ego can be utilised in situations of self-denial, co-dependant relationships and trusting prematurely, while Buddhi can be used in situations of compassion, connection and big picture thinking.

I had a secure corporate job that I was advancing in very quickly. My pay was double what people my age earned. I got to travel the world, fly business, stay in five-star hotels and eat at the fanciest restaurants everywhere I went. I made multi-million dollars deals annually, and I was good at it. But in my gut, I knew that something was missing. I knew in my heart of hearts that this was not what I was meant to be doing with my time, and I knew that I was supposed to help people.

I was a responsible mother. I did not have the financial means, the experience, nor a concrete logical reason to quit a job like that, virtually overnight, and pursue my dream of opening a space where people could heal. Yet, somehow, I knew that this was exactly what I had to do. The voice in my gut said there was no other way, and it was a sure voice. This was one of the first instances when my inner voice spoke so loudly about a decision so big. My spiritual work had fulfilled its purpose: to un-cloud the voice of Buddhi.

There was no fear in my mind about this decision. It was quiet, and therefore, there was no ego. My heart knew that I was doing this for both myself and others and that there was no other way. This is what happens in our most peaceful moments in life when we feel connected instead of separated. In those moments, because we are connected, we are not concerned with our own interests or Ego; we experience a feeling of unity and completeness. This is the state in which our desires are completely peaceful and aligned with the wellbeing of everyone and everything. When we live in this state, life becomes harmonious.

> "Use me, God. Show me how to take who I am, who I want to be, and what I can do, and use it for a purpose greater than myself."
>
> – Oprah Winfrey

Erich Schiffmann describes this in his article "Listening for Guidance" when he says that we are like drivers driving a car and can only see a few miles ahead and therefore unaware of any upcoming traffic jams. But imagine having a helicopter that can see the whole picture. This helicopter can detect and prevent us from being stuck in a traffic jam. If the helicopter had a radio signal that gave this information out all the time

(Buddhi), then all we would have to do was to tune into the radio station that broadcasted that information. But we wouldn't hear it if the radio was off or if we were listening to another channel (Ahamkara).

What we are not

There's a humorous story told by Mooji: a man goes to the doctor and says, "My whole body hurts." The doctor, looking perplexed, asks the patient to explain what he means. The man lifts his finger. "When I press here, it hurts", he says, pressing on his arm, "and when I press here, it hurts", he said, pressing on his leg, "and when I press here, it hurts", he winced, pressing on his cheek. This went on for some time. The doctor looked at this patient and said, "Son, your finger is broken".

I found that often it seems like we have many problems, but when we dig down, there are a few points from which our perception was modified and caused our suffering. The finger in this story represents the mind or the Ego. It was vital for me to look at my mind because it was the one bottleneck, the one point from which all my perceptions had to come through.

Trying to fix everything on the outside that was not going my way was both impossible and useless. There was just too much, and I had very little control over what happened outside of me. Obtaining the things and people I believed would make me happy was impossible both to achieve and sustain. And even the things that I did manage to achieve did not bring me the happiness that my mind promised, not for long anyway. It was now up to me to find another solution. Mindfulness gave me a way to work on what was happening inside of me. I did not have to change the whole world; I just had to change the standpoint from which I was thinking of and seeing the world.

The problem is not that we have a mind; the problem is that we believe we are the mind. I remember when my teacher drilled "you are not your mind/you are not your thoughts" into me, and it made me so confused. If I am not my mind, then what am I?

We are programmed to identify with our thoughts so much that we are not sure what would be left without them. And if we believed that we are our mind, then how are we supposed to have space from it, have a say away from it, believe anything other than what our mind tells us.

At some point in our childhoods, humans buy into the false definite separation of "me" and "others". We begin to believe that we end where our skin is and that others begin where their skin does. This separation begins to show up as identity, ideas and feelings. Identity sounds like: I am a girl, I am short. Ideas sound like: I am Arab, I am Muslim. Feelings sound like: I am angry, I am disappointed. Children begin to compare their looks, toys, talents and friendships to one another. This comparison then translates into a thought, "My shoes are better than hers", or "Her shoes are better than mine", or "I wish I had her shoes" and so on. In Yoga, this experience of separation is referred to as the Ego or "Ahamkara".

The ego, in simple words, is our belief that our mind, body and emotions are what we are. Let's examine this for a moment. When you ask someone who they are, they say "I am Mohammed", or "I am Layla" and so on. They will say

"I am male/female" or "I am a teacher", they will say "I am an animal lover", "I am a cancer survivor" and so on.

Contrary to common belief, the Ego is not the enemy; it was originally created to serve us. For example: when our body is hungry, the ego will say, "This body is hungry, I am hungry", and so we find a meal to eat. If we come to contact with a lion, the Ego will say, "I am in danger", and so we will start running and so on. However, we get in trouble when we believe we are the Ego. This intertwining between who we are and what our mind says means that we remain trapped in the demands of a mind that changes its mind all the time. Without training, the mind keeps a person shackled into a narrative that isn't being questioned or examined.

The Ego is a very limited way of identifying ourselves. It is choosing a part of ourselves over the whole. One thing I advocate is that we are everything. We are both honest and liars. Hardworking and lazy. Even male and female. This broader acceptance of the gradient of the human experience allows us to take in, nurture and integrate all parts of ourselves into one whole that works in unity for our wellbeing (more on this in the Therapy chapter).

Not only is identifying ourselves with our Ego limited, but it is also harmful as it can bring with it suffering. If someone, for example, strongly identifies with "I am a wife" and then becomes a divorcee or a widow, then there will be a great deal of suffering. The nature of the human mind is that it looks for consistency in order to feel security, but nothing is permanent. If we identify ourselves with the Ego, then we are identifying ourselves with something temporary.

Our age, physical appearance, social status, health, relationships and beliefs are all subject to change.

The Ego also creates suffering through comparisons. I suffered as I compared how restricted I felt in a married life and being a young mother with the freedom my single friends had. I suffered as I compared how my metabolism changed in my thirties in comparison to how it was in my twenties. The Ego compares the way we feel to the way others feel; for example, "She has a much happier life than I do". The Ego also attaches to certain feelings. When we are happy, the ego says, "I always want to be happy".

When we are sad, it says, "I don't want this. I want to be happy". While there is nothing wrong with both feelings, and while arguably being happy is preferable to being sad, it is unrealistic to expect that we would be happy all the time, nor is it beneficial to resist sadness where it is a natural feeling. Feelings are fluctuating and changing all the time.

If we are not the ego, not the mind, not our thoughts and not our body, then who are we?

"Who am I?" This is the ultimate question of all spiritual teachings. Mohammed (PBUH) went into solitude to get answers in the Heraa cave in Makka, and the Buddha sat under the Bodhi tree for many years and asked, "Who am I?" amongst many other great saints, prophets, teachers and self-realized beings that managed to reach Truth.

The concept of understanding that I am not who I always thought myself to be can be very unsettling. During my Yoga Teacher Trainings, I remember my teachers kept asking us to look beyond the ego to find a "place of silence" and to know that this silent witness is who we are. And I remember that at that time, it sounded like gibberish. It also sounded unappealing; silence sounded empty, like I will be losing out if I went there. I knew who I was, I knew what my role was in this life, how others saw me, how I saw myself, and I knew what I liked and what I didn't.

After all, if I am not my body, then why do I get so upset by how much it weighs? Or more extremely if I was to lose a limb? If I am not my thoughts, then why do I take the voices in my head so seriously? Why am I driven by my ethics? If I am not my emotions, then why are my experiences coloured completely by the emotion I am feeling in that moment?

The short answer is: I have a body, I have thoughts, I have emotions. To have something means you own it. There is an owner and the owned. When we look at the reflection of our bodies in the mirror, we never say, "That is me"; we say, "That is my reflection". The word "my" indicates that there is an object that is being observed by the subject. In the same way, "my body", "my thoughts" and "my emotions" are being observed by a subject that is beyond those objects.

If we imagine that just for a moment, we are able to shelf away our "personality", the combination of our identification with our mind, body and emotions, we will find that we are still here. If, for a moment, you drop your idea of who you are, you will find that there is a sense of witnessing presence that is watching everything unfold without being affected by it. A part of us is living the drama, identifying with it, while another part is the watcher, the listener, the witness.

This silent presence is a part of ourselves that has always been there and remains unchanged. It is the part that the creatives refer to when they feel immersed in their creativity, that "it wasn't me" that did that painting/dance/wrote that poem, etc. In some traditions, this is called the Soul or the Self. This is not something to be imagined, for if we were to imagine it, then it would just turn into another thought, another belief system and remains unhelpful. This is something that needs to be experienced. Once we are able to drop our identification with the ego and experience this presence, it becomes easier to feel peaceful in difficult moments.

Identity is a big part of the struggle of the borderline. I have found that identifying with the witness has been a great help because the witness is consistent even when the Ego changes. The witness also provided a secure base to go back to when feelings were heightened and it was difficult to self-soothe. Understanding that there was a part of me that was alright, safe, unchanged even when there were other parts of me that lived in a tornado gave a level of comfort that I craved and needed.

During my divorce, I was in contact with my Yoga teacher, Lucy, who is a compassionate and empathetic human being. Responding to her email, I wrote: "I feel lost. I know God is grooming me for something larger than I can see now, but I feel so sad." To which she responded, "Your faith is admirable & will surely carry you through this fire." This ability to see beyond our emotions and thoughts is not only faith. This is a witnessing presence that I experienced in my thousands of hours of mindfulness practice. I have seen how that presence remains calm. This is why the practice is important. It is practice for moments like this, where you are in desperate need of an all-encompassing awareness that knows it remains untouched by even the most traumatic experiences.

It is possible to identify Ego-driven thoughts because their behaviour is predictable. It is important to point out here that there is no need to fight with the Ego because when the Ego is "caught", it almost acts like a toddler that had been caught doing something naughty; it stops. Fighting with the Ego, entertaining it or believing it gives it power, and so it acts up. Whilst, in reality, the Ego is like a mirage; when you recognise it's an illusion, it disappears. Here are common themes of Ego-driven thoughts that cause suffering:

- Thoughts of separation: People are out to get me. Being defensive. Absence of feelings of belonging. Being unable to feel loved. Disconnecting from how others feel. Conflict and confrontation. Judgement: feeling superior or inferior to others.

- Low self-esteem: negative self-talk, comparisons, sacrificing oneself, ignoring own feelings and needs, putting oneself last.

- Judgement: of oneself or others. Concepts of "better" and "worse". Limited thinking and putting things into boxes.

- Dissatisfaction: thoughts of "could be", "should be", "would be" and "must be". Sense of lack. Resistance to the present moment.

Mindfulness in practice

To be mindful is to bring your whole mind into the present moment. It is the practice of noticing your body, your thoughts and your emotions at any given moment. To be mindful is to be awake to the now regardless of the disturbance of the internal dialogue of the mind.

It's the practice of pausing, take an inventory of what is occurring now. When I was with the Bramha Kumaris on Mount Abu, a bell would be rung a few times a day. We would know that meant to pause in remembrance, bringing our whole selves, body and mind in remembering God.

Mindfulness is the antidote to dissociations. Dissociation is escaping a painful experience; it is the opposite of presence. What I noticed as I became more mindful even of dissociation was that I began to know when I was dissociating and therefore was able to bring myself back more quickly. I would pause mid-conversation with friends and go "hang on, I'm dissociating", bring myself back, then continue.

The ancient traditions of mindfulness as well as the latest research in mindfulness practices most effective for trauma[2] are presence, affect and perspective. Each one of those practices is effective in its own right. Together, they have been found to be most effective for trauma recovery.

---

[2]Trauma research by Tania Singer et al from Social Neuroscience Lab, Max Planck Society, Berlin, Germany.

Presence

The practice of presence relates to bringing your mind to something that exists in the present moment, namely the breath, the body or a repeated phrase (mantra).

An example of breath practice is the spinal breathing we saw in the spirituality chapter. In the same way, repeating a phrase (such as Aum or any word that touches you, such as "joy" or anything else at all) gives the mind one thing to focus on. A third practice is to hold your attention on the body either by focusing on one spot (such as the heart space) or consciously moving your awareness to specific body parts, one at a time (for example: starting from the toes and moving up to the head, or focusing on one of the seven chakras[3] at a time).

As you do this, your mind will wander into thoughts that are not related to your point of focus. When this happens, you can turn your attention back to your point of focus as soon as you notice the wandering of the mind. With time, your identification with thoughts reduces, and so it loses its power over you (remember, you're sitting with your best friend, and the TV is running in the background).

However, I have noticed that in the beginning, there are some strong and recurring thoughts that are difficult to ignore. Sometimes, it is better to go full throttle into those thoughts instead of brushing them off. Doing the opposite,

---

[3]Chakras are energy centres in the body. I will leave it up to you to research those as it is outside the scope of this book but to simplify the seven main chakras are the: crown, third eye, throat, heart, solar plexus, sacral and root chakras.

thinking completely and strongly of those thoughts until there is nothing left to be thought of, can be useful. An enquiry you can explore with when it comes to those thoughts looks something like this:

- Is this thought completely true?
- Is it true all the time?

Is there a way for me to be sure?

- Are there instances in which this thought is not true?
- When I stop believing that this thought is completely true, how do I feel?
- What do I become when I drop this thought?
- What would happen if I stopped believing this thought?
- What would I be without that thought?

For example: Say you have an argument with your partner. You begin to say to yourself, "My partner doesn't care about me. All he/she cares about is him/ herself". When you ask yourself if that is completely true all the time, you will find that it is not. You will say, "Actually, that's not true, my partner took care of me when I was sick, he/she paid my phone bill last week, he/she even made me dinner the other night. I choose to believe that my partner cares about me because that makes me happy and loved". When you find specific examples that discard the belief system, it becomes easier to replace a thought that creates suffering with one that creates unity, compassion and happiness.

This is particularly helpful to the borderline as the thoughts move into black-and-white, all-or-nothing thinking.

I had always felt that people that show up late to an agreed time of meeting are disrespectful. But that thought had ruined many meetings and outings for me. It was only till I decided to believe that people were not intentionally late to offend me but rather because they have time management issues that I felt more peaceful with late people. I still believe in the social responsibility of respecting time. I just feel that I have more choice and power in my reaction now.

The other way mindfulness can be practised is somatically (using the body). This can be done in stillness or in movement such as Thai Chi, Yoga, intuitive dancing or even a walking meditation. To tune our attention to the way our bodies feel. Explore:

- How does my body feel in this moment?
- Where exactly do I feel this feeling?
- Is it tight? Heavy? Hot? Expanded? Light? Etc.?
- Have I felt this feeling before?
- If my body could express itself clearly to me, what would it ask me to do?

The borderline struggles to self-regulate, to calm down feelings when they are disturbed. And working with the body rather than the mind is very effective when there are no words or easy ways to explain how we're feeling. I find shaking, jumping, stomping, sighing, pushing, and even punching (not humans, pillows) are particularly useful.

I have also found that exercising regularly (and a Yoga practice) helps me feel stress, resistance and hyper-arousal in my body. I "feel" when I need to get my body moving, and that makes it easy to choose the right type of movement depending on the situations. Sometimes, I need a slow, grounding walk, other times, I need a challenging resistance training session, and at other times, I need a creative Yoga flow or dance.

Affect

Affect is the practice of empathy and compassion. The borderline is empathic by nature. Our ability to feel for someone else, as if their pain is our own, is inherent. A part of that comes from the blurred lines of boundaries that were experienced in childhood. Compassion is a skill where we feel for someone without getting too involved. The skill of compassion means that you are able to project loving-kindness (Metta) onto another person while activating the centres of joy, love and connection in the brain.

I use the word "skill" to describe compassion because it is a resource that can literally save the life of the borderline. Our ability to feel compassion not only to others but towards ourselves can help in resolving many of the borderline challenges, especially when it comes to shame and guilt. We saw the practice of metta meditation in previous chapters. Feel free to use this practice or any other practice that activates the emotional energy for your own wellbeing.

Perspective

There's a zen story about a young Buddhist, who on his journey home came across a wide river. He stared hopelessly as he contemplated a way in which he could cross the river. Just as he was about to give up, he saw a Zen master on the other side. He yelled over to the master, "Oh wise one, can you tell me how to get to the other side of this river"? The teacher ponders for a moment, looks up and down the river and yells back, "My son, you are on the other side".

Perspective is the ability to stand in someone else's shoes and imagine their experience in a certain situation. As a borderline, I have found that sometimes feelings are so hyper-aroused I find it difficult to think from a point of view outside of mine. This is when perspective can give the space I need away from my own narrative. Here's how:

Remove yourself from the story: When you are suffering with a certain thought, imagine that the situation that is causing your suffering is happening to someone else (that is not too close to you) that you are trying to soothe. Listen to the kind of advice you'll give this person.

OR

Set up two chairs facing one another, one is for you and the other is for the person you are in conflict with. First, take your seat and say out loud all the things that you are thinking and feeling. Do this until you have no more to say. Then, take the seat of the second person, imagine what they would say back to you, make this as realistic as possible. Return to your seat and argue back. Continue to do this until you have a better understanding and more compassion for the other person.

> "The mind before meditation is like a cup of muddy water. If you hold the cup still, the mud settles and the water clears. Similarly, if you keep quiet, holding your body still and focusing your attention on your object of meditation, your mind will settle down and you will begin to experience the joy of meditation."
>
> – Bhante Gunaratana

Here's my grey when it comes to mindfulness:

Mindfulness is the ability to check in with ourselves. Since the borderline both loses a sense of self easily and suffers severe mood swings often, this is an invaluable skill. It gives us the ability to pause before we react, curb impulsiveness when it strikes and provides an internal map that we are missing most of the time.

I find that as a borderline, and as a therapist, being able to articulate our experiences is a near-impossible mission in the state of high arousal. Practising mindfulness is like exercising a muscle; it gets stronger the more it is practised, making it possible to control, manage and choose our reactions with time.

What is also helpful about mindfulness is it helps differentiate the internal work from the external work. What I mean is that by bringing the mind to the present moment, you can clearly see "This thought/emotion is not about now, this is an old wound that I still need to heal" vs "This is not okay in my reality right now, I need to change something on the outside too".

> "Where would I find enough leather To cover the entire surface of the earth? But with leather soles beneath my feet, It's as if the whole world has been covered."
>
> – Śāntideva

7 Therapy

I have no doubt that we are just starting to understand borderline and that we have a very long way to go. The stigma around borderline is strong, and the sooner we get educated on it, and the more willing (and hopefully excited) therapists are to work with borderline, the more lives will be saved. According to Clearview Women's Center of Borderline Personality and Emotional Disorders:

- Six Million Americans are diagnosed with BPD.
- That is double the diagnosis of bipolar and schizophrenia combined.
- Ten per cent of people diagnosed as borderline commit suicide.

Borderline's early experience for me was chronic depression. By chronic, I mean there was not a time in my adult life where I did not feel depressed. Yet, I hid my illness so well. I hid it from my family for a long time and even from some of my closest friends. The experience was isolating and painful. In the instances where I opened up, I found myself in situations where I was given unsound advice. Friends and family said things like "Thank God for your blessings", or "Look at all the good things in your life" or "You need to have more faith in God". Their advice is well-intended, good-hearted and severely irrelevant. Mentally, I understood their advice, but during the depths of my depression, none of that resonated; this has made me feel ashamed, invalidated and alienated even more.

My first encounter with therapy was when I was twenty-five. A combination of postpartum depression, suicide and anxiety made it clear I needed help. I wanted help. I think that was a very important differentiator. If you speak to anyone who has recovered from depression, they would tell you that they only recovered because they chose recovery, sometimes with the help of others, but they did it. They got sick of being sick and chose, by their own means, to bring themselves out of it. I am blessed to have come across helpful, intelligent, compassionate and understanding people along my path to recovery, but I am soberly aware that I had done all the work. That there was no way for me to be helped if I did not want to be helped.

The first psychiatrist I saw diagnosed me as bipolar. Given I had manic episodes followed by depressive episodes made it obvious why he mixed me up with a bipolar. He put me on an anti-depressant and a mood stabiliser.

I hated it. I felt like a zombie, my manic episodes were gone, and I was left with a dull, monotone existence that lacked the invincible, excited breaks I got from my manic episodes.

I saw a second psychiatrist. I was now diagnosed with "bipolar personality" and depression. The diagnosis shocked me, especially the depression part. Wasn't everyone this sad? I have been more or less this sad all of my life, was it just me?

This one spent more time with me, validated my feelings, perked up my self-esteem a little, changed my medication. Tranquillisers were added to the cocktail.

He also put me on a "truth serum" in one of our sessions, a medication I was injected with that kind of put me in a trance. The aftermath of that session was traumatic, to say the least. I felt raw, disoriented, abandoned and hyper-aroused.

The tranquillisers I was on had the side effect of inducing suicidal thoughts on some people. I was some people. After a few months, I took twelve times the dose of tranquillisers that I was prescribed. Many people, even those who have known me for years, do not know this about me. I have only recently started talking about this, actively de-stigmatising mental illness and suicide (still considered a crime in some countries, including my own).

Before that, I have skilfully managed to put on such a happy, strong and successful front that no one suspected a thing. I grew so good at concealing my sadness that even my parents were shocked when I told them I was on anti-depressants. I hid my sadness with humour, my loneliness with hard work, and my vulnerability with a sharp tongue.

I felt both helpless and hopeless. I had no reason, no will and no energy to live. I was angry with my parents for bringing me into the three-dimensional world when I had not been consulted on the matter. Nothing in my life felt like "me". I was frustrated with how little control I had over my life.

After that attempt, I went off the meds, cold turkey. I remember clearly sweating in my bed, no one around me. I hadn't developed the skill of being vulnerable then, and I chose the wrong people to be vulnerable with. This was when the cutting became my only relief from the emotional pain I was in. I wish I had support to go through that experience. I felt alone, lost and very sorry for myself.

One of the biggest obstacles I had to overcome after that was my inability to accept the parts of myself that I did not like. I saw my whole self as those parts, and I loathed myself. I felt deep shame that froze me, I did not love myself, and I could not imagine anyone loving me if they knew the "real" me. I now know that the only way I can change anything I dislike about myself is to first accept myself as I am now.

This was when I turned to meditation, then energy healing, then Yoga. I had a system in place that literally saved my life. I was empowered, I had a choice, I had a plan, and I started loving myself.

For eight years, this system worked. I held on to it like my life depended on it because it did. I knew what (most of) my triggers were. In some ways, though, that system was fragile. It was also very black and white; there was only one way for me to do this, and I could not see beyond it.

After my divorce, I felt uprooted. My whole support system crumbled, or so I urged it to. In my hyper-arousal of processing a major transition in my life, I saw abandonment even where it did not exist. My desperate need for support landed me in a relationship with a narcissist who sucked the life out of me. I started cutting again. After yet another incident of gas lighting, I was triggered beyond repair. I drove to a pharmacy, bought a box of anti depressants, kissed my daughter goodbye, and left to end my life. I took half the box, put on some music, and waited to die. This was my second suicide attempt. I was back at square zero.

The narcissist showed up, found out I had attempted, laughed at me, and left. I was found by a family member and ended up in a hospital. I was interrogated by a police officer who informed me that in order to receive any medical treatment, he would have to register my "crime" of attempting suicide. Great. Not only did my life suck, not only did I suck at suicide (second fail), but I am also now a criminal. I signed an AMA (against medical advice) and left the hospital without receiving the care I needed. My stomach was not pumped. I lived with tremors that lasted months after that.

I left that hospital, I ended up in a private hospital that only administered sedatives to prevent me from attempting again, which I had made very clear that I would, and I meant it. I was a wreck. Every day I woke up with the dread of having to endure yet another day. I wailed at the thought of having to live through another sunrise, and another sunset. I did not want to participate in life. I resented my parents for bringing me into it. This was the lowest point I had ever been in, in years.

At that hospital, I received my borderline diagnosis. The

relief I felt was immense. There were finally words to the experience of being me. I was not alone! Other people lived in the hell I lived in too. Misery loves company.

I am glad I got diagnosed, but I'm not saying it was easy. The literature around borderline is not exactly charming. And to be told that you see the world through the lens of your "disorder" means that you begin to question your role in all the failed relationships and friendships over the years. I replayed some scenarios in my head, I had to make some amends with people I pushed away, and I did in my journey of recovery.

I often wonder if my journey after being diagnosed would have been easier if my world was not falling apart. The gas lighting[4] that comes from narcissistic abuse makes anyone question reality. To be questioning reality because of my disorder, on top of that, was a hellish cocktail.

I started the recommended treatment for Borderline Personality Disorder: Dialectical Behavioural Therapy (DBT). DBT can be very effective for some people with borderline. I was not some people.

I stuck with the treatment for months, showing up religiously to my weekly sessions. Meanwhile, the narcissist re-entered my life. I felt worse after each therapy session. I am not saying it did not help me at all; it did. Understanding that there are alternative explanations to people's behaviour besides "They don't love me", "They will leave me" and

---

[4]Gas lighting is the technique used by narcissists to manipulate people into doubting their own sanity and sense of reality.

"I'm not good enough" was useful. It did not work for me. Here's what I believed happened:

Firstly, most of the issues I was bringing into the therapy room related to the narcissistic relationship I was in. DBT encourages ownership of our feelings, which is great. Most of my reactions in that relationship, however, were somewhat normal, borderline or not.

Secondly, it had an undertone of blame, which pushed me further into shame, which kept me frozen, debilitated and unable to deal.

Thirdly, as a borderline, I needed validation of my feelings, normalisation of my experiences and security within the therapeutic relationship, which did not exist.

Fourthly, Borderline Personality Disorder is a trauma response. Trauma requires work with the body and not only the intellect. Feeling forced to change my behaviours and thoughts rather than having my feelings compassionately looked at felt even more isolating and forced.

Fifthly, DBT is a journey of self-enquiry, which I had been doing for nine years by the time I ended up in that therapist's office. It assumes lack of introspection, which was not the case here.

The effect of narcissistic abuse is devastating. More so on the borderline. The narcissist plays at the fears of the borderline by creating experiences of abandonment followed by empty promises rigged with gas lighting. This makes the borderline feel even more unstable than normal.

After a few months of this, I gave up therapy altogether. I dumped the narcissist, and I was back to square zero once more.

The months that followed were very similar to a PTSD response. I was triggered by anything that reminded me of the abuse that I had lived. Being vulnerable was out of the question. I could not even hold eye contact without experiencing full panic.

I was resentful towards the thousands of hours I had spent in practice of Yoga, meditation and self-enquiry. My black-and-white thinking was heightened, saying "None of it worked, none of it matters, just give up".

I struggled to work; I felt uninspired in a job that required constant inspiration. Having to remain in the role of a caregiver both as a yoga teacher and mother made me feel sick. I could hardly take care of myself. I felt like a fraud, an imposter, a failure.

I was angry. I was angry at myself for buying into the lies of the narcissist, for not having better judgement, for bending all the rules for a person that did not deserve it. I was angry that this monster got away with ruining my hard work. I was angry that nothing was working anymore.

I salute myself for having a tiny shred of hope amongst all of this despair. I reached out to a friend who recommended Eman Nourridien, an experienced therapist that has had success with borderlines. I requested an appointment to resume my DBT therapy.

The therapist calmly explained that although DBT works

for some people, she had other plans for me and asked me for a chance to work using the tools that she had applied successfully with borderlines. Her regimen included hypnotherapy, parts therapy, somatic interventions and attachment therapy.

This journey was both painful and rewarding. Unlike my previous experiences, this therapist was compassionate, validating, normalising and solid. It took just a few sessions for me to trust that she knew what she was doing.

Through hypnosis, I discovered what dissociation was. Regressing back into my childhood years, the child version of me was impossible to connect with. In the hypnotic state, she would disappear, grow too small, or too big. My subconscious mind protected me from the pain of becoming a child again. When it finally happened, I broke down completely. I had pushed that version of me so far back into my mind I refused to be her. It is hard to describe the process of associating; it does not translate well into words, like trying to get someone to understand your dreams. What I can say about it is, it was painful as hell. But what followed it was what I could only describe as embodiment. I finally learned to be my Self, in my body.

There was a lot of reconciliation that happened. Parts therapy, simply put, was like getting the different versions, aspects and facets of you to work together rather than against each other. Accepting all the parts of me, including the wounded child, including the suicidality, including the self-harm, including all the parts of me that I have outcasted, ignored, forgotten about and shoved down, was a refreshing change from the self-improvement mentality that I had unaffectionately forced on myself for years.

Attachment therapy was about giving me experiences of safe, attentive, consistent, enabling relationships. Those were encouraged by vulnerability, trust, self-esteem, my relationships started changing, I started rebuilding bridges and repairing ones that I had so skilfully destroyed. It was the start of building a community through a support group that I created mainly for myself.

The other intervention that my therapist introduced that translated my highly cognitive experiences into embodied ones was intuitive dancing. There was something about dance that not only made me feel safe in my body but also gave me flashes of insight into myself that were not intellectual but rather experiential, making them much more effective in bringing about growth, change and understanding.

Here's my grey when it comes to therapy:

I have put in a lot of work, and I still have a way to go. It hasn't been easy, but it has been rewarding. I still have blind spots, and there are still things that I would love to tidy up. I still catch myself in distress, muttering, "I wish God would just take me". In the meanwhile, I have finally stopped seeing suicide as a solution. Cutting is no longer appealing. I feel more like myself today than I ever have, and although I know that growth is not linear, I feel more comfortable in my own skin every day. have been misdiagnosed, mistreated and misunderstood. But all of those turns, although they seem to have made my journey harder and longer, landed me where I am today, and for that, I am grateful.

The mind can only take us so far. There is also great power and healing both in the subconscious mind and in the body that is often overlooked. The hardest path is not always the best path. Sometimes, compassion, connection and congruence is all we need.

I dream of a world with more therapists willing and competent to work with borderlines. I dream of therapies for the borderline that are compassionate, inclusive and understanding. Of a world where the stigma of having borderline is eradicated enough for a person to receive their diagnosis and be okay with it. I dream of the word "personality disorder" to be removed. Nothing is wrong with my personality; it's just that inside me lives a very scared little girl.

As a borderline, it is easy to ignore the small successes, but those are like pieces of a puzzle; you get handed a piece, one at a time and one day, the pieces begin to fit together better, and it starts to make sense, it starts to feel better.

> "It is bad enough that you were robbed of your childhood- it is unacceptable to lose the present and the future."
>
> – Judith Herman

8 Surrender

It is vital for me to speak of surrender because without it, I don't think I would be here. My experience has taught me that you can only go so far with effort; the rest of the way is pure grace.

This is a core teaching of spirituality of many traditions. Surrender is understanding that and trusting in a force that runs the world in harmony. You can call that force God or something else; it does not matter. This is the consciousness of the universe that keeps moving it towards the best possible outcome of love in every second.

The way I see it is that the macrocosm of the universe is reflected clearly in the microcosm of the human body. If you think about the human body, for example, regardless of how we treat it, what we label it, what we put in it and where we take it, it is always looking to heal, so is the universe. If we eat something that poisons the body, it throws up and gives us the runs until the poison is out. In the same way, the universe is operated through this intelligence that is constantly looking to heal. The symptoms of the healing (throwing up/runs) might be severely uncomfortable. Trusting the discomfort as a process of healing can provide the resilience and meaning we need when things get tough.

Surrender is not being idle, not making plans or being passive. Surrender is active, determined and clear participation in the present. Often when I talk about surrender, my students ask things like, "What should I do?" I encourage them to think of surrender as an internal process, not an external one. It is about how we react internally more than what we do externally. It is an internal knowing and trust that on the large scale of things, it will all work out. There's a difference between not studying for an exam and studying hard for an exam then getting a question you did not expect or prepare for. Do you then resist, blame, and create internal and external conflict? Does it help? Does this false sense of control serve you in any way?

During the transformation I felt when it comes to my relationship with God, I started thinking of God as super mom or super dad. Mom/Dad loves me so much, always has my back, and is always looking out for me. Even when I have preferences and desires, even when I resist anything that runs against my plans, even when I am frustrated and sad, there is an undertone of knowing that I am taken care of that has changed the way I look at the world. The more gracefully I connect to this knowing, the easier my life feels.

When we have surrendered, when we allow our desires to be absorbed in Divine order, our life flows with ease. When there is trust in our hearts that things will turn out okay, we lose so much of the anxiety we carry around. When we are not rigidly attached to a preference, our lives continue to be both exciting and fulfilling.

The more aligned we are with the source, the less self-centred desires we will have. We become more easy-going, surrendered and trusting in that whatever is at the moment is the best possible scenario. The absence of desire will therefore mean that we will be getting what we want all the time. Surrender offers a direct way into self-realization. It is not a passive act; it is an active choice of allowing.

Surrender in Spirituality

My spiritual teacher, Amma, portrays the beauty of surrender in a small story: The person on the spiritual path seeking God is like a little child seeking his mother. This child will be busy playing with different toys, and so the mother will playfully go and hide. Once the child is done playing with his toys, he will go and seek his mother. He will run into the living room and not find the mother. He will then run into the kitchen and ask the cook, "Have you seen Mother?" and the cook will say no. The child will then run out into the garden and ask the gardener, "Have you seen Mother?" to which the gardener will respond with a no. While the child is applying all this effort to find his mother, the mother is playfully watching as the child is trying to locate her. But the mother will only reveal herself from her place of hiding when the child gives up, sits down on the floor and cries for her. It is then that she will appear to hold the child in a warm embrace.

In the same way, the spiritual seeker applies effort to find God. He does rituals, prayers, chants and gives offerings, but it is not until he realises that it is by Divine grace that he will find God that he does.

There is another story told by Amma of a salt trader that went out to sell his salt. As he was heading to his destination, the sky poured down, and all his salt dissolved. He was devastated but decided to get some rest as the night fell. While he was sleeping, he was ambushed by bandits who demanded he hands over all he made that day. The trader swore that he had sold nothing as the rain melted his salt. The bandits did not believe his story and threatened him with guns. When they tried to pull the trigger, the guns did not shoot as the rain had ruined the gunpowder. The trader's curse is now his blessing. The same rain that ruined his merchandise saved his life.

The strange thing about surrender is that we sometimes find it easy to surrender ourselves to someone other than God. We trust that certain people can take care of us and would never do anything to harm us, and in many cases, that trust is valid and worthy. But we do not have the same faith in the one that created it all.

> "It is by surrendering the limitations of its own banks that a river becomes the mighty ocean. Do not be afraid to throw away the trinkets of your ego to gain the diamond of grace."
>
> – Swami Veda

Surrender in Life

Motherhood, to me, had been the biggest teacher of surrender that I had ever encountered. I see myself as a very reliable, organised and punctual person. Having a baby had taught me the hard way that being open to a plan B is the easiest path. As a young, inexperienced and impatient mother, I found it frustrating that overnight, I had no control over my time—or life for that matter—anymore. The simplest of tasks, such as going to the grocery store, seemed to be an impossible task that felt like I was running in my own spot for hours. I would get my baby ready, and after rushing to dress myself, I would find that she had soiled herself. I would then have to stop and get her changed, only for her to start crying out in hunger. After having to sit down to feed her for a minimum of half an hour, she would fall asleep, which held me hostage from moving a muscle as I knew how agitated she would get if I woke her up. By the time she woke up, it was too late to go out.

I also had no control over my energy, I felt tired, and that had meant that I could no longer do all the things I found easy to do before. My body did not feel the same, and physical activity had to massively change. Travelling was tricky, and it was very much dictated by this supremely cute and yet life-altering person. The frustration I felt over losing complete control over my life was one of the best lessons I had. In those moments, I could either choose to rigidly attach to a schedule that wouldn't work (or ideas of how my life, body and energy should be), or I could accept that I had very little control and make the best out of what I was experiencing. Only one of those options brought with it peace and joy.

There is an old Taoist story that demonstrates this. There was a wise farmer that grew crops for many years. One day, he woke up and found that his horse had run away. The neighbours heard of the unfortunate news and came to console him.

"What bad luck," they said.

"Maybe," replied the farmer.

The next day, the horse returned, bringing with it ten other wild horses. The farmer now had eleven horses instead of one. The neighbours came to congratulate him.

"What good luck," they said.

"Maybe," replied the farmer.

The Farmer's son attempted to tame one of the wild horses, fell off the horse and broke his leg. The neighbours heard the bad news and came to check up on the boy.

"What bad luck," they said.

"Maybe," replied the farmer.

The day after, military officials came to their village to recruit young soldiers. They took one look at the farmer's son and decided not to take him as he was injured. The neighbours heard of this fortunate coincidence and came to congratulate the farmer.

"What good luck," they said "Maybe," replied the farmer.

Surrender at work

Surrender is where all creative energy emerges from. You see painters, musicians and dancers perform arts that seem superhuman. Many of them will report a feeling of not having control over their creative work, that it simply "came through them". This is what happens in surrender. Even work can be an active practice of surrender. Deborah Adele, the author of The Yamas & Niyamas: Exploring Yoga's Ethical Practice, says that surrender is about "Getting off stage and putting God on there instead".

There's a difference between having a plan but being open to all possibilities of how it will come about and being rigid and fixated on how we want things to unfold. When I proceeded to set up a space for healing back in 2011, I had my heart set on doing Reiki healing on people. I wanted to share the practice that saved my life with others. When I went to register Namaste, the Yoga studio I still run, I was told that all commercial registrations that were to do with alternative therapy were frozen while committees decided what was eligible for commercial registration and what was not. I had quit my job and wanted to start healing as soon as I could. I thought for a while and decided that, since I liked Yoga, I would get certified as a teacher and do a few classes a week, just as a front, while I took on clients that needed healing for the rest of my time. Kind of like one of those supermarkets in New York, with the poker table in the back.

After Namaste opened, there was very little demand for Reiki and a reasonable demand for Yoga. Because I was so attached to Reiki, I did not see then that Yoga might be my path. That God is granting me the wish of helping others heal, but with a tool that I was more fit for. After many months of struggling with getting Reiki clients and having my capital nearly wiped out by rents and bills, I threw my hands up in the air and said, "God, make this work". I surrendered my desire by accepting that I needed to focus on teaching Yoga. I made a vow of spending more time on becoming a better Yoga teacher and on not taking on more Reiki clients until I felt a strong sign from God. Doing that was a turning point for my studio. It boomed, people knew about it, and classes finally started filling up.

When I teach Yoga, I find that I exhaust myself when I teach with my mind, and I find that classes simply flow through me when I surrender the outcome. When my mind is quiet and my heart is receptive, I find that I do not mind what I teach and how. I do not mind what sequence I'll teach and if my students will get the postures right. All I feel is that God is guiding me to provide exactly what is needed in that moment. My mind's preference does not make a difference. In those classes, teaching is effortless and joyful. "I" am not teaching. "I" am simply allowing the teaching to come through me.

There is a story about a fat king and his wise advisor. The king consulted his advisor on all matters and never went anywhere without him. They often went riding on their horses to discuss important matters. The advisor always provided valuable and wise advice to this king. The advisor was well known for accepting situations and making the best out of them always. One morning, as the king got out of bed, he fell, and his elbow split open. He yelled at the advisor, demanding he explained why his elbow was hurt and how he would manage running a kingdom with a hurt elbow. To which the advisor responded:

"Your majesty, this is also good."

"Good? You call this good?" yelled the king, frustrated and in pain. His agony and anger drove him to order the guards to throw the advisor into the palace dungeon.

Weeks passed, and the king's elbow slowly began to feel better, and so he decided to get on his horse again. He rode for hours and hours, then sat under a tree to take some rest before heading back to his palace. What he did not realize was that he was so absent-minded during his ride that he had passed the borders of his kingdom and come into a town of cannibals. He awoke to a group of those cannibals tying him up and preparing his fat, juicy body for supper.

The king was terrified, preparing for his own sad end. At the village, the cannibals noticed that the king's elbow had a bandage on it. The cannibals were disappointed; they cannot sacrifice an imperfect human, regardless of how juicy he looked. The king was so relieved and finally understood the advisor's words. He rushed back to his palace, having prepared an apology for his advisor.

"You were right all along; it was good. I am sorry I didn't believe you. I understand how this was good for me. But tell me, do you think you being locked up in here was also good?"

"Yes, Sir, it is also good," responded the advisor.

"Good? What do you mean good?" the king was confused.

"If you had not thrown me in the dungeon, I would have been with you on that ride, your majesty. They would have seen your infected elbow and released you, and I would have been their supper," smiled the advisor.

Surrender at selfless service

Even the most noble work can be surrendered. Preferring to be used in God's service regardless of our personal preferences is surrender. I spent ten days up in the mountains with the Brahma Kumaris, a spiritual group that practices Raja Yoga. I listened to their teacher Dadi, a selfless saint, describe her experience as someone who completely surrenders to God. She said, "Sometimes Dadi finds herself in London, and Dadi is thinking what is Dadi doing in London. And then Dadi meets some people, and they need help, and then Dadi knows what she is doing in London". She continues to say, "I am Baba's (God's) puppet".

When I visit my guru in India, I carry sweets, biscuits and other treats for the children in the village. I hand those out as I come across children on my way to prayer or when I volunteer in the school. On one of my trips, I filled my bag, as I always do with treats. However, I felt that there was a little bit more determination than the usual flow I felt while I was there. On that particular day, it felt as though the children disappeared from the village. I looked and looked but there was no one to serve. The teaching of my guru came strong, in silence and yet as clear as day, as it usually does: to serve others is not a virtue, it is a privilege. It is only by grace and surrender that we are granted the gift of serving.

The teaching of karma yoga (the yoga of action) tells us that service itself is the reward, not the outcome of the service. Our job is to show up and do the work, not to control the outcome. It is easy to feel overwhelmed and powerless when we look at all the things that need to be "fixed". Approaching life, one foot in front of the other, with determination and joy for being able to serve, gives us purpose and power.

Here's my grey when it comes to surrender:

Surrender is hard, especially when the world does not feel safe. The catch 22 is that surrender itself is a practice of safety. To think that out there, there is a higher power, a more precise intelligence, a loyal friend that can and will take care of me is a game-changer, especially for the borderline.

My invitation is not to surrender to be a good person; it's not a moral higher ground. Think of it as a healthy coping. I was having a conversation with a highly intellectual Yoga teacher that I respected. He mentioned to me that there were three attempts that would have ended Hitler's life before he caused all those deaths. All those attempts were failed by natural causes. What made me believe that there was a God? My answer to him was, "I believe in God because it feels good to me. The world would be too scary if I didn't. I like to believe that there is an intelligence that knows more than me, knows the future, knows the big picture. It feels safe to know that God's got this." Whether you call this God or Love or The Universe won't matter much; what will matter is the feeling and state it brings you.

> "Sometimes surrender means giving up trying to understand and being comfortable with not knowing."
>
> – Eckhart Tolle

9 Relationships

A borderline child learns, through neglect or threats of neglect, abandonment or threats of abandonment, that they are not good enough. Sometimes, the caregiver or caregiver's behaviour is directly contributing to this learning. In other cases, the conclusion that the child makes is the child's understanding of the situation, which might be incomplete at that developmental stage. The effect of that understanding is traumatic in both cases.

The reason children choose to make the conclusion that they are not good enough instead of thinking that the parent is not performing well enough is this: it feels safer for the child to say, "I am the problem, I can do something about it, I will fix it, then things will be OK" than to say "My main caregiver and the person responsible for my wellbeing is broken". The latter thought directly affects the child's sense of survival and safety.

And when I look at the symptoms of the borderline, it all adds up. Here is the narrative I believe most borderlines will relate to most of:

I don't know who I am because my boundaries were

never clear to me. What I needed did not matter. I was not sure if I was the child or the caregiver. Separation from my caregiver was so painful I never learned where

I ended and where my caregiver began. The separation from my caregiver is because I am not good enough.

If I am not good enough, then I will continuously try to reinvent myself in the hopes that one day, I will find a version of me that is lovable, acceptable, that will make people stick around and love me. But because I don't truly believe I am lovable, I never arrive at that version.

Because I am not good enough, I will do everything I can to keep people around; I might come across as needy, or overbearing, or overly attentive. I will idealise the person I believe will relieve me of this painful feeling that I am never going to be able to connect with anyone, not in the long term anyway.

This belief that I am not good enough is so ingrained in my belief system that it feels dangerous for me to think otherwise. So even when there are no signs of abandonment, I subconsciously create the perfect conditions for my belief to materialise: I push people away, I shut people out, I sabotage relationships, I ask unreasonable things just to find truth that I was right all along: no one can love me long enough, not when they know me anyway.

It's not that I don't want close, intimate, safe and nurturing relationships. There's probably nothing that I want more. But there is also nothing that scares me more. The trauma of being abandoned again is bigger than my heart can hold. It feels too risky for me to be vulnerable enough, to open up enough, to get close enough to feel the pain of not being good enough again.

There has been great relief for me when I chose to walk away. The anticipation of being abandoned is finally relieved, and therefore, the anxiety subsides when bridges are burned, even if those bridges are ones that I want, value and wish to keep.

Abandonment is the thing that scares me the most. I lose a lot of control when I am triggered by that fear. I tell myself lies that I then tell others in what seems to be manipulative behaviour. It's not that I'm lying to you; it's that I'm lying to me too. The fear makes it difficult to see clearly. I don't lie because I lack empathy; I probably have too much of it. But the fear of the pain of abandonment overrides my logic, my ethics and any sense of control I have over my behaviour.

I feel too much at times and need to numb it down. I feel too little at other times and need to feel alive again. I feel most alive when I do something impulsive that reassures me that I am still here. It's hard for me to get a sense of myself. I struggle to feel or know who I am when I'm lost in that fear.

This feeling that the floor beneath me is unstable is unsettling, to say the least. To feel all this pain and experience it as a lonely and painful journey with no one to help me with this burden can become overwhelming. Suicide is a valid option when you have lived with this constant pain for years. It has been a valid answer for many of the problems that overwhelmed me over the years. It gives me a sense of strength, that I have a choice, that I am in control.

The world feels scary and lonely. It is difficult to hold abstract ideas, not have clear answers or deal with the anxiety of the unknown when I am triggered. The easiest way for me to create certainty in such a scary world is to resort to black and white thinking. Black and white is certain, clear, definitive. It becomes the source of stability when the world is falling apart. The thought "Although you hurt me, I still know you love me" is a very difficult concept to grasp. Those two truths cannot be held in my mind, not without work.

I have never felt secure in a relationship. How am I supposed to recreate security when I have never experienced it? I am filled with jealousy watching people continue to be friends with their childhood friends while my life seemed to recycle all relationships that meant anything to me.

My understanding of the reason for this narrative is this: security in relationships is something you learn at some point in your life, most likely during childhood. Secure relationships are similar to walking or talking. Imagine if a child was never taught to walk or talk, or if the child wasn't allowed to. Or if the child thought they weren't allowed to and no one corrected that understanding. That skill would be missing for the child.

The borderline never got the chance to practice security in relationships. They find themselves, as adults, missing this crucial part of their development. This missing part creates so much suffering, but there is no way for the borderline to catch up with what other adults in their lives can do so easily without practice.

So my message to those who care for or love a borderline is this: please help them practice security. Prove to them that you want to stay, that they are worthy of your love, that you are not going anywhere. I am in no way underplaying the pain, effort and energy it takes to care for a borderline. You can use a therapist as a mediator and engage in active self-care. If the borderline in your life is open to change, then your presence can be a crucial part of their recovery.

Sometimes, it is difficult for someone with borderline to establish healthy boundaries. This is because their own sense of self is not solid. Because the borderline likes things to be in black and white, setting very clear rules and boundaries (that you both agree on) will prove very useful.

Idealisation and Devaluation

The black-and-white thinking of the borderline spills into the relationships that matter the most. A person is either a saint or a sinner, with not much in between. The borderline desperately searches for security and intimacy in relationships and therefore idealises the person they believe will "save" them from their painful experiences. I often think of how I had made people feel at this stage, it must be so alluring to have someone view you as perfect. How easy it is to fall in love when the person you are with sees you as this perfect creature.

This of course does not last. The borderline then finds out that this person is human, and inevitably, flawed. In a way, this is a reenactment of the way the borderline experienced the caregiver; they "should have" been perfect, they "should have" made things right, but they didn't. This was followed by an awakening that the caregiver makes mistakes which, as we saw before, makes the world a dangerous place.

It took me time to be able to hold both truths. I still catch myself looking for flaws in people I admire. Only now, I use their flaws as proof that they are human rather than a reason to shut them out forever. A story

that really helped me grasp the idea that we're not perfect, but we're also not all bad is told by a Buddhist monk by the name of Ajahn Brahmavamso that taught meditations in prisons in Australia. After conducting a few meditation sessions, the prison officer in Perth called him to ask for him to come back to teach meditation. Upon apologising due to prior commitments and suggesting to send a colleague instead, the prison officer insisted that Ajahn must visit the prison once again. When Ajahn enquired on why the officer insisted that he came himself, the officer said that he had noticed that something that had never happened before had started happening after Ajahn's visits. The prisoners that learned meditation with Ajahn never came back to prison again. This meant that those prisoners had learned to be a part of the outside world, leaving behind the violence and crime that is often taught in jails.

Ajahn Brahm believes that the success of his courses happened because, unlike most of us, he did not see those prisoners with the same labels most of us see them with: rapist, thief, drug dealer, murderer. He saw people who committed these crimes but never labelled or identified them with the crimes. He does not believe that labelling a person with one act that they committed is fair. He also does not believe that thinking of people this way is helpful as we are re-enforcing that image in the minds of people who had committed crimes, making it more difficult to dis-identify themselves from their crimes.

Ajahn explains that he had come to this conclusion because of the story of the two bad bricks in the wall. When Ajahn had moved in with other monks into the new monastery that he lives in now, he had to become the builder. The job of laying bricks was a precise and lengthy process. He laid this great wall of a thousand bricks with mindfulness and dedication. When he was done with the wall, he stepped back to admire the wall but had found that there were two crooked bricks at the centre of the wall. For three months, looking at that wall made him sad. He had nightmares about it and avoided showing people this wall that reminded him of his mistake. Until one day, one of the elder monks looked at the wall with admiration and praised it. Ajahn was surprised by this comment and pointed to the two bad bricks that, to him, had obviously ruined the wall. But the elderly monk responded with, "I see the two crooked bricks, but I also see the 998 good bricks". This changed the way Ajahn looked at people as even those who committed some of the worst acts also committed many good ones.

Similarly, a tradition from the Babemba tribes of southern Africa practices radical acceptance and forgiveness. When a tribe member makes a mistake, he or she is placed in the centre of a circle of all tribe members. For several days, tribe members begin to recite all the good qualities they know about that person, allowing for change in the perception of all tribe members, including the one who had made the mistake. They recite with as much detail as possible all the good things this person has done. This is because everyone, even those who committed terrible mistakes, has a good side to them. When doing so, the person is then reminded of their good nature and are encouraged to nurture this part of themselves. This is the polar opposite of being in a society that labels us with something we resent in ourselves. This causes us to identify with that label and continue to act upon it.

I find those stories particularly helpful in this book for both the borderline and those that love one. Separating the action from the person is vital for the success of relationships for and with the borderline. The borderline needs to take a step back from seeing the person as the two crooked bricks. The one who loves the borderline needs to see the person underneath the childhood trauma. For the borderline to gain security, they need to know that someone, anyone, will stick around, no matter what.

I think the first time I experienced this security was when I met my guru. The second time was when I met my last (and current) therapist. Experiencing security for the borderline gives them the muscle memory to recreate this relationship with other people too. Sometimes, all they need is that first (or second) relationship in which security is completely experienced for the healing to kickstart.

Triggers

It might be helpful to outline some common triggers of the borderline. Gaining insight into those triggers will help the borderline separate the symptoms of the disorder from reality. It might also prove insightful to those who love a borderline and often struggle to understand intense reactions. I find most triggers fall into one of three categories: powerlessness, shame and terror.

The following triggers relate to feelings of powerlessness or loss of control:

- Being surprised
- Having to wait
- Being asked a lot of questions, especially by authority figures
- Being threatened
- Feeling trapped
- Being told what to do

There are also "not good enough" triggers that often bring about shame:

- Being alone
- Failure to follow through
- Disappointing people
- The "silent treatment"
- Being happy/unhappy
- Feeling guilt, shame
- Being centre of attention
- Feeling inferior

Triggers that affect anxiety and terror:

- Anger and angry expressions
- Parents yelling at their children
- Dark rooms

- Change (bad or good)
- Being watched
- Witnessing others being hurt (can also be under powerlessness)
- Heights
- Confrontation

The Repair

What some parents reading this book might begin to think is: what if I screwed my children up? Am I not allowed to make mistakes? Am I completely responsible for the way my kids turn out to be? The answers are: you will screw up your kids anyway, you are allowed to make mistakes, and no, you are not completely responsible.

If you notice all the TV shows that portray a pretty good family system, from Full House to This is Us, you will find that it is not that members of those family did not make mistakes; it is that they have an excellent way of repairing the damage.

My personal journey tells me that the borderline has not experienced good repair within the family system; this is what makes it difficult to imagine that someone will stick around after a conflict. This is why the borderline has resigned to the idea that all relationships end.

This experience of conflicting between "I can't afford to screw up because there will be no repair" and "There is no point trying because I will screw up and it won't be repaired" is a very lonely and isolating one. It makes sense then to explore the science of Yoga, as a science that promotes oneness and connection, for a remedy for this experience.

Yoga provides us with a four-fold remedy to all the distractions that block us from experiencing the oneness. Those remedies (Patanjali Yoga Sutras from Chapter 1 sentence 33) are as follows:

1. **Maitri—friendliness** | Feeling love towards those that are easy to love. This love is unconditional, similar to a love of a mother. With this love, even enemies can turn into friends.

2. **Karuna—compassion** | Compassion is different from sympathy. Sympathy is feeling sorry for another being. Compassion is the ability to see the point of view of the other.

3. **Mudita—delight** | Feeling joy for the success of others. Similar to compassion, it is experiencing the other's feelings, of joy or success, as our own.

Upeksa—disregard | This is dismissing the two crooked blocks in the wall. This might be the solution to the borderline's famous rage. Disregard does not mean acceptance of wrongdoing. Instead, it means understanding that most people are trying their best, most of the time.

> "Your heart is the real temple. It is there that you must install God. Good thoughts are the flowers to be offered to him. Good actions are worship. Good words are humans. Love is Divine offering."
>
> – Hugging Amma

10 A Life Worth Living

For most people, to want to die, you would need a pretty good reason. For the borderline, the opposite is true. The borderline's default is the desire to die; it is living that is debatable.

I find the borderline's pessimistic view of the world is arguably a more accurate representation of reality than that of non-borderline persons. Here's why: I read in Neel Burton "Depressive Realism" that most non-depressed people view the world through rose-tinted glasses. This means that, for example, most people will over appraise themselves as better drivers, parents or citizens than the average. This, by definition, negates the idea of "average". Mentally "healthy" people are not focused on the possibility of divorce, death, illness or having an average child. Those "positive illusions" keep people pro-life instead of pro-death. It allows for risk-taking, resilience against traumatic events but can also cause disappointment and failure.

On the other hand, the borderline knows: we are too small to make a big change, this constant run of life is meaningless, we're all going to die in the end, so what's the point? Life brings us misery, and people hurt us.

But accuracy is not always the point. The hope that humans have are key for resilience, enthusiasm, creativity and power. For the borderline to have a desire to live, I will tackle the three basic emotional needs according to the self-determination theory (SDT): autonomy, competence and relatedness.

Autonomy

Autonomy to me has been about the ability to self-define, self-regulate and self-depend.

Self-defining is my ability to sense myself and who I am. For many years, how I saw myself was purely dependant on what others said to me and how they saw me. I was too distracted by the outside, what everyone was doing, how everyone was feeling that there was no space for me to feel who I was. My ability to know who I am took the practice of self-acceptance (I meditated on loving myself and consciously took actions of self-love), boundary setting (I learned where my responsibilities end and how to say no) and ownership of my body (by learning to connect to my body and learning to listen to the signals that my body sends).

Ironically, self-defining has also meant the ability to accept my instability of self-image. To take that part of me that is constantly changing and also accept it as a part of who I am.

Self-regulation gave me power over what thoughts I choose to give my attention to, how feelings pass through me, and how I behave based on those. I never thought I had any say over how I felt. Emotions were too overwhelming and powerful for me to feel like there was a decision-making part of me that could get a word in edgeways. The combination of meditation, mindfulness training, Yoga and DBT awoke that power within me. That power meant that I actually had a choice over how I saw things. When someone looked away while I spoke to them, for example, it could mean that they didn't like me (old interpretation), or it could mean that they were preoccupied (new interpretation). Both interpretations might be inaccurate (unless clearly stated by the other person). But now, I choose the inaccurate interpretations that feel better for me.

Self-regulation also meant learning to soothe myself when my feelings were heightened. I practised both soothing myself alone and doing it with another person (co-regulation). I learned that there is a time and place for either and that both skills were important. Both played a big role in building stronger, more intimate and longer-lasting relationships.

Finally, **self-depending** meant that I stopped looking for a hero that would save me from the pain I was living in. I learned that everything I changed in myself I had to do myself; no one could do it for me. Others can help, guide and support me, but I did it all in the end. I went from being co-dependent to being hyper independent, to finally being able to achieve interdependence, being in relationships that honour both individuality and the ability to connect bravely with someone else.

Competence

What I want to add to competence for the borderline is meaning. I did well in school, I did well as a programmer, and I did well as an account manager. But I was not doing well inside. It all felt empty. And while I felt a certain amount of happiness when I got validation for doing well in things that I knew how to do well, it was short-lived. What I understand today is that there was a yearning inside of me all along. That yearning was to be able to help and connect with people. Our yearnings are all different. To me, teaching yoga, psychotherapy and volunteer work has fulfilled that yearning. I do not imagine that my life would have been the same if I was not fulfilling that yearning every day. My involvement in something bigger than me gives me a good reason to get up in the morning and do my part, even on days where depression, resignation and hopelessness peaked its head at me even before I got out of bed.

This meaning is what fuels us to do better, to be better, to go against the odds even when things seem tough. Meaning does not have to be noble nor big. It just has to speak to our hearts strongly. Meaning is what gets us excited and willing to participate in life. We all have individual talents, callings, abilities and resources that support this meaning. This can be in the form of excelling in a job we do, making a difference in the world or simply the ability to express who we are and what we stand for.

Relatedness

We need to belong. We need to feel that we are a part of something. I looked for relatedness in romantic relationships thinking that was the only place I could find it. What I had learned is that there is an abundance of beautiful, caring, loving people to connect with. The feeling of loneliness I was feeling was not because of lack of people around me; it was because I was too afraid to open up. I had mixed up intimacy with romance.

I now know that holding an eye gaze longer, giving someone your full attention, and even being romantic with non-romantic partners (think buying flowers for friends) can fulfil that. I have found the closeness I was seeking being vulnerable, telling my story, holding someone's hand while they grieved, listening without interrupting and seeing people, and myself, for who we are.

Final Thoughts

If you do not have time to read the whole book, here it is in a nutshell:

- Borderline personality disorder is the result of childhood trauma. A person with BPD is not dangerous, difficult nor untreatable.

- The culture around borderline needs to change if we have any chance at saving the lives of the borderlines. I believe the stigma around borderline contributes to the loneliness and isolation that drives the suicide.

- If you have a borderline in your life, remember this: when triggered, you will be dealing with a child who is scared of nothing more than being abandoned. If you wish to build intimacy with this borderline person, you will have to make sure (sometimes hundreds of times) that they understand that nothing they can do or say will push you away (and boy, will they test you). This will be hard at times; practice self-care.

- That "treatment" for borderline is as individual as the person. My own journey taught me that working with the mind, the heart, relationships and spirituality were all essential for my ability to experience security and clarity.

What I have learned in the past thirteen years, from the time I started working on myself to the time of writing this book, is this:

It is possible to hold two opposing truths at the same time: to say a parent could do everything in their power to take care of and protect a child and for the child to still feel neglected.

That most of the truth lies in the grey, the space between two extremes.

That I am more powerful, resilient and beautiful than I give myself credit for.

That when it all goes to shits, I chant "Om Namo Narayani" I surrender to God. That I feel in my heart and in my bones that I am loved, protected and safe.

That within me is a place I can always retreat to, connect with and recharge. That place is safe and complete, and it's the launching pad from which I can help others.

That I forgive myself for the many ugly things I have done and all the people I have lost. I did not know better, so I could not do better. Now I do, and I have every intention of doing better.

That borderline is part of me, but it is not me. There is more to me than meets the eye. What was once a demon that controlled my life is now a scared, small part of me that shows up when I'm not doing too great, but I recognise it as such. This allows me to take ownership of reactions related to my disorder with people around me. We have a deal, me and this little monster. It gets to speak, but I have the final say.

"The Middle Path is an alternative to the sort of thinking that becomes locked in extremes....Rather than offer a compromise between such opposing views, the Middle Path posits that neither extreme represents reality. When one rejects attachment to the extreme, what remains is the true nature of things. Therefore, the Middle Way is not a passive state of middle of the road thinking. Rather, while recognizing and rejecting limiting or biased views, it is an active state of developing the wisdom to perceive the true nature of things and to act accordingly."

– Daisaku Ikeda, contemporary Buddhist teacher

Acknowledgements

To my mother, for showing me that with a good heart, it is possible to be better, no matter what your past was.

To my father, for seeing the best version in me even when I couldn't.

To my sisters, for being my mirrors, my backbone and for calling out my bullshit when I needed them to.

To my daughter, Sahar, for being my longest standing guru of unconditional love, patience, wonder and beauty.

To my Guru, Amma, for knowing me completely, and loving me anyway.

To my best friend, Deema, for teaching me secure attachment.

To every student that made me teacher and every teacher that made me student. To everyone that took that internal journey within themselves and helped me do the same. To everyone that wanted to die and decided to stick around. To the people that loved me, the people that challenged me and the people that damaged me, I would not be here without you.

Made in the USA
Monee, IL
10 September 2021